Between Mango Trees and Maple Leaves:

A Memoir of Finding Home Between Continents

Saanvi Kishore Thakur

Qurate
quratebooks.com

BETWEEN MANGO TREES AND MAPLE LEAVES:
A Memoir of Finding Home Between Continents
Saanvi Kishore Thakur

Published in 2025

© Published by

Qurate Books Pvt. Ltd.
Goa 403523, India
www.qurratebooks.com
Tel: 1800-210-6527, Email: info@quratebooks.com

ISBN: 978-93-58985-59-7

Dedication

To all global citizens and travelers – those who bridge cultures and bring the world closer, living the timeless truth of Vasudhaiva Kutumbakam, meaning "the world is one family." May your journeys and connections continue to reflect this ancient wisdom from the Maha Upanishad, reminding us that across borders and differences, we belong to one global household.

Preface

My story is one of frequent shuttling between two countries—India and the United States of America. I've never stayed in one place long enough to feel like I truly belonged. But maybe that's the point—belonging isn't about where you stay; it's about how you carry the places you've been.

I was born on October 16, 2011, and most of my childhood was centered around New Delhi, India's capital city. I grew up amidst a lively, dynamic atmosphere—traffic horns, street vendors, and people who always seemed to be in a hurry for almost any activity!

My school was in Gurgaon, a city on Delhi's outskirts that seemed to grow taller and shinier every year.

My family's roots stretch across villages and cities in India. My dad's hometown is Bokaro, an industrial city in the state of Jharkhand, where the air smells of steel plants and ambition. My mom's hometown is Darbhanga, a city in the state of Bihar. It's quieter, marked by old traditions. Then there's the village of Padri, also in Bihar—our ancestral roots—where our grandparents came from. It's a place where people live in community structures and follow norms that would be the envy of many affluent cities around the world.

Every year, I've had the chance to spend two weeks away from Delhi and Gurgaon and experience a change of scenery in Padri, Darbhanga, and Bokaro, staying connected to my family roots.

In 2018, my life shifted gears. We moved to the United States of America—a change I never fully saw coming. But I adjusted over time. We landed in Ellicott City, Maryland, a suburban town that was comparatively quieter in ways Delhi never was. Life slowed down there.

When the slow pace began to feel a bit sluggish, we'd often visit Baltimore or Washington, D.C., both less than an hour's drive away—trading the calm of home for the energy of city life. Baltimore's rough edges and Washington, D.C.'s polished monuments couldn't have been more different, yet both added to the mix of experiences shaping my idea of "home."

A special moment in my life came when my younger brother was born on October 16, 2021. We share the same birthday, which makes our bond even more special.

I've shuffled between India and the United States of America frequently. This book is about the pieces of myself I've left in each place. It's about Bokaro's steel-fueled drive, Darbhanga's traditions, Delhi's constant chaos, and Ellicott City's quiet rhythm. It's also about the in-between spaces—Gurgaon's contradictions, Baltimore's grit, and Washington's grandeur. These places aren't just dots on a map; they've shaped how I see the world and my place in it.

Through these pages, I want to show what it means to move, to adapt, and to grow in a life that never stops shifting. As I grow, I look forward to learning new things, meeting new people, and experiencing new places.

It's not always easy, and it's rarely simple, but it's the story of how I've found fragments of home in every step.

- Saanvi Thakur

Contents

Part I

Delhi: The Chaos of Contradictions

Delhi has always been home for me. I was born and brought up here. Nestled in the northern part of India, it's India's capital city that wears its history on its sleeve. From the ancient stones of the Red Fort to the bustling lanes of Chandni Chowk, there's a certain energy that pulses through every corner. There's something about the constant hum of life—whether it's the crammed metro stations, the never-ending traffic, or the warmth of the people—that makes it feel like the heart of India.

Welcome to the Heat Zone

"You step out of the airport, all cool and calm, like you're in a movie, and then—bam—the heat greets you like an old friend who hugs a little too hard. It's like stepping into a warm oven. The air wraps around you—not in a cozy, blanket kind of way, but more like the sweaty side-hug you didn't ask for. My shirt is already sticking to my back, and the pavement feels hot enough to fry an egg.

I glance at my sister, who's already tying up her hair, silently plotting an escape to someplace cooler. Meanwhile, my baby brother is grinning like this is all one big cosmic joke. He's probably already made peace with the heat, forming a secret alliance with it. My mom, composed as always, takes the lead and flags down a cab with the focus of someone on a mission.

The air is thick with the scent of car exhaust, sweat, and street food sizzling in corners you can't quite see—food you're tempted to try even if your arteries protest. But somehow, the smell is familiar. It smells like home. In 2018, we moved to Ellicott City, Maryland, USA. And now, in 2022, after four years, we were returning to Delhi.

We make our way to a beige cab—because of course, it's beige. The car equivalent of "I've seen things, but I'm still rolling." My dad is already deep in fare negotiations while the rest of us linger around like background characters in a slow indie film.

The cab's air conditioning hums to life, clearly trying its best. It's not much, but it's enough. My sister exhales like the heat had personally offended her, while my brother keeps up a cheerful babble, blissfully unaware.

The ride is a kaleidoscope of honking horns, glowing shop signs, and buildings that look like they've weathered a thousand monsoons—and are ready for a thousand more. Delhi's streets are a living, breathing contradiction: sleek sedans gliding past stray cows, neon boards clashing with peeling paint, tradition woven into every corner of chaos.

It's a lot to take in—but you can't look away. After all, this is home. And what's a homecoming without a little sweat, some chaos, and a whole lot of heart?"

Delhi Belly: A Culinary Rollercoaster

But then, as if on cue, the most typical 'Delhiite' of all questions, bubbles up as we pull into the driveway: "What are we eating?" Because, of course, in this city, food is never just food. It's a conversation, an argument, an identity crisis all rolled into one. And today, like clockwork, it starts with something traditional. Lunch is what lunch has always been: a home-cooked reminder of where we come from, as though mom is determined to anchor us with every bite.

Daal (a dish made with lentils or other split pulses) bubbles on the stove, *rotis* (flatbreads) puffing up like small, golden clouds as mom moves around the kitchen with the kind of efficiency that's almost surgical. My dad hovers, tasting and adjusting, as if this meal is a science he's determined to perfect. He approaches the *daal* with the seriousness of a scientist defusing a bomb, adding a pinch of salt with a flourish like it's a secret ingredient no one else knows about. My sister mutters under her breath, "As if that salt is going to change the entire universe," but my dad ignores her.

We sit down, and for a while, everything is quiet, grounded. The food is simple—*daal, rice, sabzi* (cooked vegetables)—but it tastes like home. The kind of meal that feels like a warm hug and an unsolicited lecture from an elder all at once. This is what it means to be here, in this house, with this family, in this city. It's like time pauses, just for a second, as we eat in the kind of silence that's more comforting than any words could be. Well, until my brother breaks it by trying to dunk his *roti* into his water glass.

But this is Delhi, and the peace never lasts. Because by the time dinner rolls around, the indecision sets in. The city's confusion about its own identity bleeds into our dinner choices, like we've spent all our decisiveness on lunch and now, faced with the limitless possibilities of modern Delhi, we're utterly paralyzed.

Someone—probably my sister—suggests pizza for dinner. I can almost hear the collective groan, but then, because this is who we have become now, after having lived in the USA. Someone else suggests pasta. And then the spiral begins. What about Chinese? How about burgers?

At one point, my dad pipes up with, "What if we just reheat the *daal*, which we had for lunch?" and the way my sister and I simultaneously glared at him could have powered an entire grid! It's like the city is in our blood, making us incapable of sticking to anything. We end up doing what we always do: ordering everything: pizza, pasta, and some biryani for good measure. Afterall, in Delhi, food isn't just about hunger; it's about options, about excess, about embracing the chaos.

My mom then adds a salad to the order, for "balance," and we all know no one's going to touch it except maybe my dad, that too out of guilt.

The plates on the table are a mess of cultures and cuisines—half-eaten pizza slices sitting beside *naan* (a slightly puffed flatbread) and leftover rice, pasta tangled in the same bowl as yesterday's *sabzi*. My baby brother gleefully creates what he calls a "fusion masterpiece" by sticking fries into his biryani, announcing proudly, "It's modern art!" My dad pretends not to notice, probably to preserve what's left of his sanity.

My sister's busy trying to make her pasta look Instagram-worthy, holding her phone at an angle that requires her to practically climb onto the chair. Meanwhile, my mom sighs and mutters something about "kids these days" before stealing a piece of garlic bread off my plate.

And as we sit there, picking at the remains of this confused dinner, I can't help but think about how this is the most authentic Delhi experience! It's a city that doesn't know what it wants to be, a place that refuses to settle, that thrives on contradictions and indecision. One minute, you're rooted in centuries-old tradition, the next you're drowning in a sea of globalization, wondering how you ended up here. But somehow, it works. Somehow, in all that mess, in the indecision, there's something beautiful.

We finish dinner in silence, not out of any particular reverence but because we're too tired to argue anymore. My brother is happily mixing his pizza with his rice, blissfully unaware of the culinary crimes he's committing. My dad finally cracks and says, "You're going to ruin your digestive system," but my brother just grins like a miniature Gordon Ramsay who knows his creations are revolutionary.

My mom? She's watching us like we're the sitcom that never ends. And in the quiet aftermath of the meal, it hits me: this chaos, this indecision, this beautiful, frustrating mess—this is our home.

And maybe that's the real secret of Delhi. It is almost obscene in its indecisiveness, but at the same time, it feels like the only logical outcome in a city that refuses to be defined by one thing. It's not about grand gestures, traditions, or modernity. It's about the space in between, the contradictions that somehow, impossibly, make sense. It's about not knowing what you want, but being okay with that, because in the end, it's the journey that matters more than the destination.

Lohri in Delhi: Where Tradition Meets Bollywood

Lohri is a harvest festival celebrated primarily in Northern India, marking the end of winter and the beginning of the harvest season. It is celebrated predominantly by the Sikh and Hindu communities. The festival takes place on January 13th each year, marking the culmination of winter and welcoming the longer days of sunshine as the sun moves towards the Northern Hemisphere. Celebrations include bonfires, music, and dance.

Lohri in Delhi is nothing short of a spectacle—a dizzying blend of tradition, modernity, and the inevitable chaos that follows any festival in this city. It's as if someone handed Delhi a script for a calm, rural celebration and the city decided, "Nah, let's add some fireworks, questionable dance moves, and at least one uncle arguing over who gets to light the fire."

The festival, deeply rooted in the agrarian past, finds itself reinterpreted in the urban sprawl, where every street corner buzzes with activity, and every moment is as much about spectacle as it is about sentiment. Vendors selling roasted peanuts, jaggery, and popcorn turn the streets into sensory landmines. One wrong move, and you're caught in a spiral of "just taste this" or an unsolicited lecture about how peanuts are "perfect for winter, *beta* (son)."

My mom, always the centerpiece of our celebrations, dives into the fray with a kind of precision that borders on the obsessive. Her kitchen becomes a battleground where she wages war against the clock to ensure that everything—from the crispy *makke ki roti* (flatbread made of corn) to the rich *sarson ka saag* (dish of mustard greens cooked with spices)—is prepared to perfection. You'd think Gordon Ramsay was about to waltz in for a taste test with how she's barking orders at anyone who dares enter her domain. "*Beta* (son), if you're not chopping, stirring, or grinding, you're in the way!"

My father, on the other hand, is the unsung hero of the evening. His role is more subdued but no less significant. As dusk settles, he's out by the bonfire, carefully arranging the wood with the precision of someone who's secretly googled "How to make a perfect bonfire," but won't admit it. There's something almost meditative about it.

My older sister, meanwhile, is already immersed in the social whirl of the evening. She's a social chameleon, effortlessly navigating between friends and family with her phone permanently glued to her hand. She's snapping pictures of the food like she's being sponsored by *#Indian Cuisine*, but let's be honest, the only thing she's uploading is a highly curated shot of her outfit captioned *"Lohri vibes."*

And then there's my baby brother, a human sugar rush who sees the bonfire as a challenge. He starts chucking random sticks into the fire like he's re-enacting a medieval siege. His laughter and boundless enthusiasm add a layer of innocence to the festivities—or they would if he wasn't constantly testing how close he can get to the flames before someone yells, "Stay back! This isn't a superhero origin story!"

The bonfire itself is the star of the show. It's an urbanized version of what might have been a modest blaze in a village setting, now transformed into a towering inferno that could probably signal planes.

We gather around it, tossing *rewri* (sesame seeds) into the flames, but let's be real: half of us are doing it wrong. My brother decides to lob in a handful of popcorn, sparking an impromptu family debate about whether the ancestors would approve. Spoiler: they wouldn't.

The fire's crackling is accompanied by the booming beats of Bollywood remixes that echo through the night. It's *Lohri*, but let's make it DJ night. The *dhol* (drum) beats merge seamlessly with the latest chart-toppers, creating a mashup that only Delhi could love. My sister drags me into the center of the impromptu dance circle, where I'm immediately subjected to what can only be described as the Desi Electric Slide. Somewhere in the crowd, an uncle with suspiciously energetic moves proves that the phrase "dance like no one's watching" doesn't always work in your favor.

As the night wears on and the fire begins to die down, the crowd starts to thin, leaving behind a trail of peanut shells, popcorn kernels, and enough selfie sticks to equip a small army.

My father's contented sigh and my mother's relieved smile signal the end of our *Lohri* festivities. My baby brother, now covered in soot and inexplicably sticky, declares it "the best *Lohri* ever" before promptly falling asleep on the sofa. As I watch the last embers flicker out, I can't help but feel a mix of nostalgia and amusement.

In Delhi, *Lohri* is a dazzling spectacle, a celebration that captures the city's dynamic spirit. Sure, it's loud, chaotic, and sometimes hilariously over-the-top, but that's part of its charm. It's a reminder that even in the midst of all the chaos, tradition somehow finds its place—right next to a selfie stick and a playlist that includes both *dhol* beats and remixed Punjabi rap.

Delhi's Shopping Scene: From Luxury to Chaos

Shopping in Delhi is a mix of extremes—the polished order of malls and the chaotic vibrance of bazaars. Delhi's malls, are modern and efficient. They offer air conditioning, organized stores, ample parking, and clean facilities. Shopping here is easy but expensive, often making you second-guess your purchases. Leaving during peak hours can be frustrating, with long waits to exit parking lots.

There are bazaars for shopping too of course, such as Chandni Chowk and Sarojini Nagar, but are crowded and noisy. My mom thrives here, negotiating prices like a pro and uncovering great deals. These markets are overwhelming yet rewarding, offering affordable finds and unique items. But the art of bargaining is not for everyone.

Our family shopping trips reflect these contrasts. My mom seeks the best bargains in bazaars, while my dad opts for the structured comfort of malls. I'm left carrying bags, amused by my baby brother's antics as he switches between obsessing over toys at bazaars and dismissing them once he's in high-end stores. His candid comments, like pointing out overpriced items, always add humor to the day.

Shopping in Delhi goes beyond purchases. It's an experience shaped by its settings—from the organized malls to the bustling bazaars. Every trip ends with tired feet, lighter pockets, and plenty of memories.

Delhi's Drama: A Cast of Thousands

Delhi is a city of contrasts, where ancient ruins stand beside modern skyscrapers, and frenetic street life coexists with quiet enclaves of privilege. The city's residents navigate a complex reality shaped by ambition, survival, and fractured trust. The elite live in a world of luxury, their high-rises and exclusive venues projecting wealth and success. Beneath the surface, however, they face unrelenting pressure to maintain their status. Relationships are often transactional, and social gatherings serve as arenas for subtle competition. Despite the opulence, there is an undercurrent of dissatisfaction and a search for deeper meaning.

The middle class is caught in a cycle of aspiration and struggle. Their homes and social media profiles project stability, but this carefully curated image conceals the stress of constant striving. Achievements are fleeting, setbacks feel catastrophic, and relationships are frequently shaped by the need to network rather than genuine connection. Their pursuit of upward mobility often comes at the expense of personal fulfillment.

For the working class, daily life is a fight for basic necessities. Street vendors, laborers, and service workers exhibit remarkable resilience amidst long hours and minimal rewards. While their shared struggles foster camaraderie, the economic instability and exploitation they face highlight the city's systemic inequalities. The gap between their lives and the wealthier districts is a stark reminder of social disparity. The marginalized, living in slums or makeshift settlements, endure harsh conditions and systemic neglect. Their struggles are largely invisible, overshadowed by the city's more affluent narratives. Their existence underscores Delhi's deep social divide, where survival is a daily battle and progress remains an elusive promise.

Trust is a fragile resource in Delhi. Among the elite, it is often traded for influence, while in working-class and marginalized communities, distrust becomes a survival tool. This tension between trust and distrust shapes the city's social interactions, creating a fabric that is as complex as it is fragile.

Delhi's story is one of ambition and inequality, where each individual reflects the broader dynamics of a sprawling, multifaceted city.

If Delhi were a person...

If Delhi were a person, it would be a quintessentially moody teenager, a high-stakes drama wrapped in layers of complexity and unpredictability.

Delhi struts around with an air of exaggerated confidence, wearing the trendiest outfits and blasting the latest hits through oversized headphones. Its personality is a rollercoaster, shifting from euphoric highs to sulky lows with an intensity that's both magnetic and exhausting.

One moment, Delhi is a cacophony of honking cars, street vendors shouting their wares, and crowds that surge through its narrow lanes like a tidal wave. It's energy nearly palpable, its presence impossible to ignore. The city's highs are exhilarating, its vibrancy infectious—

every street corner and marketplace buzzes with life, an endless display of enthusiasm and chaos.

But next moment Delhi enters it's brooding phase, the sulky retreat from the spotlight where everything seems to slow down. It's the teenager who locks themselves in their room, pulling away from the chaos and immersing themselves in a world of introspection. The streets, once bustling with activity, become eerily quiet, as if the city is taking a moment to reflect in solitude. During these periods, the city's vibrant colors seem muted, its usual clamor reduced to a distant echo. The energy that once defined Delhi's dynamic character retreats into a more contemplative space. It's during these moments that Delhi's complexities come to the fore—its social issues, its underlying tensions, and the weight of its historical narratives become more apparent.

The city's moodiness is a reminder of its depth, its struggles, and its moments of quiet introspection amid the external chaos.

Delhi's charm as a teenager is a blend of compelling charisma and frustrating unpredictability. It's the kind of character who's undeniably magnetic, drawing people in with a mix of charm and mystery. Its charm is reflected in its ability to surprise and enchant, whether through a hidden alleyway that leads to a culinary gem or an unexpected festival that transforms the cityscape into a spectacle of color and sound.

The city's allure is in its contrasts—the grandeur of historical monuments set against the backdrop of modernity, the rich art of cultural festivals juxtaposed with the everyday grind of urban life. This teenage persona is captivating but difficult to fully grasp. It is both exhilarating and exhausting, its tendency to be both warm and aloof, a character who keeps you guessing.

Navigating Delhi is like riding an emotional rollercoaster where every day is a new scene in an ongoing drama. The city's mood swings are felt in its social dynamics, its political landscape, and its everyday interactions. One day, Delhi is buzzing with celebrations and collective joy, a high point in the city's narrative. The next, it's engulfed in tension and conflict, a low that underscores its complexities.

Living in or visiting Delhi means embracing this ever-changing landscape—a city that constantly oscillates between extremes, its energy and mood as unpredictable as a teenager's. It's a place that offers both exhilarating highs and challenging lows, a dramatic stage where every experience is amplified to match its intense personality.

In essence, if Delhi were a person, it would be the quintessential moody teenager—dynamic, unpredictable, and endlessly captivating. Its mood swings, vibrant energy, and complex charm paint a picture of a city that's as fascinating as it is enigmatic, a character whose presence is impossible to ignore and whose narrative is ever-evolving.

Leaving Delhi: From Chaos to Calm

Leaving Delhi is like finally stepping off the set of an epic drama. The city's relentless hum and pulsating chaos recede into the background.

The departure begins with a moment of quiet introspection amid the controlled chaos of the airport. Delhi's frenetic energy, which seems to pervade every corner of life, is temporarily paused. The airport, with its antiseptic calm and muted announcements, feels almost surreal. It's as if I'm being prepped for a new act, one where the city's relentless noise is replaced by the more subdued undertones of travel.

Waiting for the flight, I can't help but notice the irony of this transition.

Around me, the usual airport hustle—the clatter of rolling suitcases, the murmur of conversations, the occasional blare of a gate announcement—feels like a muted version of Delhi's constant clamor. There's a certain elegance in this temporary calm, a hint of the peace that awaits beyond the city's borders.

The departure gate is a liminal space, a threshold between the vibrant intensity of Delhi and the serene unknown. As I board the plane, there's a sense of finality, a closing scene to the relentless urban play I'm momentarily leaving behind. As the plane ascends, Delhi transforms from a bustling metropolis into a mere patchwork of lights and shadows. The city's sprawling landscape becomes a distant tableau, its complexity reduced to an abstract, almost impressionistic view. From this vantage point, the familiar chaos of Delhi's streets seems oddly serene, like a memory fading into the background.

The gentle hum of the aircraft's engines creates a soothing soundtrack to this departure. There's a sense of detachment as I watch the city's contours blur into the horizon; a reminder of the high-octane life I'm leaving behind. The view from the window is both liberating and contemplative, a visual metaphor for the shift from the city's unyielding pace to a more introspective journey.

Leaving Delhi is a moment of both escape and anticipation. The city's relentless energy is replaced by the calm of the open sky, offering a brief respite from the urban intensity. This escape is not just a physical transition but a symbolic one—a chance to step away from the city's dramatic rhythm and embrace a different pace.

What do I carry from Delhi?

Living in Delhi, with its constant buzz and blend of contrasts, has shaped who I am in ways I never expected. It has taught me not to remain passive; it pulled me in, urged me to adapt, to keep moving, and to embrace the unexpected. It's a place where everything is constantly in flux, but somehow that's what makes it so alive and I've learned to keep pace, finding my own quiet moments amidst the madness.

Delhi has also taught me that life isn't about neat, perfect plans, but about embracing the messy and the unexpected. The streets are never the same; one day filled with the heat of a thousand people, the next, drenched in a sudden monsoon.

It's not just a city; it's a feeling, a collection of all the highs and lows, the moments that made me smile and those that made me reflect.

While walking through its crowded lanes, I realized that home wasn't just four walls. Home is that place that both challenges and comforts you, at once. For me, Delhi is one of those places!

The most striking part of my time in Delhi has been how my family and I have experienced it together. We've explored the chaotic markets, indulged in street food, and immersed ourselves in the vibrant culture—each experience adding a layer to my connection with the city. Every moment we've shared in Delhi, whether it was laughing through a sudden rainstorm or sitting quietly at India Gate, has deepened my sense of belonging, not just to the city but to my family. We are woven into every corner of this place, creating our own patchwork of memories amidst its noise. And even in the midst of the overwhelming chaos, I've learned to find peace.

My family has been my anchor here, helping me navigate the unpredictability, showing me that even in the heart of the chaos, there's a way to find calm, to find your place in the world. With them by my side, I've learned that home is not just a physical place—it's the people you share it with, and the way they make even the most chaotic environments feel like home.

Delhi taught me to embrace the messiness of life, to find my own rhythm in its unpredictable beat, and to understand that, sometimes, the most beautiful moments are the ones that come out of nowhere.

Gurgaon: Mirror of Modern India

Gurgaon, located just southwest of Delhi in Haryana state of India, is a thriving city known for its modernity and wealth. It is a hub of skyscrapers, luxury malls, and cutting-edge infrastructure, reflecting the rapid urbanization and economic growth in India. The city's skyline is a testament to its affluence, offering a lifestyle that is sleek and global, with high-end businesses, residential complexes, and entertainment options. To me, Gurgaon represents a world of opportunity and success, where wealth is on full display, and the pace of life is both exciting and relentless—a city that defines the new face of modern India.

Arriving: The Tale of Two Cities and One Overachieving Cousin

The highway between Delhi and Gurgaon is the closest thing to a metaphor for that one family WhatsApp group where one cousin is a struggling artist trying to make ends meet, and the other is posting selfies from their new penthouse. Delhi is indecisive, unsure whether it wants to be the old- timer sipping *chai* (tea) or the cool millennial ordering oat milk lattes. Gurgaon? Gurgaon is the cousin who got into an Ivy League, bought a Tesla, and now refuses to acknowledge anyone who doesn't have a trust fund!

Leaving Delhi feels like peeling away the clingy layers of an ex who keeps reminding you of all the good times, even as you're trying to move on. But Gurgaon doesn't wait for your emotional baggage—it's already booked a first-class ticket to the future.

One second you're in Delhi's chaotic embrace—rickshaws weaving through traffic like drunk mosquitoes, roadside *chai* stalls spilling tea that could start its own gossip column, and streets so tangled they look like your earphones after five minutes in your pocket. The next, you're in Gurgaon, where the roads are so wide and clean they look like they've been photoshopped. Honestly, it's a bit unnerving.

Gurgaon doesn't flirt with luxury; it's married to it—and not in the cute "high-school sweetheart" way but in the "million-dollar wedding at a castle in France" way. The glass skyscrapers rise like overachieving kids at a spelling bee, their reflective surfaces showing nothing but themselves. It's like the city's saying, "Why bother with a past when you can just reflect the future?"

The trees along the roads are suspiciously perfect too, like they're auditioning for a high-budget nature documentary. I half expect to see one holding a yoga pose.

As we pass Cyber Hub—a monument to Gurgaon's commitment to bougie aesthetics—I can't help but notice that even the air here feels different. In Delhi, the air hugs you a bit too tightly, thick with the history of every secret whispered over *chai*. In Gurgaon, the air is crisp, filtered like it comes with a subscription service.

The people? They're not just living their lives; they're curating their existence. Everyone walks with the confidence of someone who's just updated their LinkedIn with a new job title.

And then there's my friend's house. Oh, boy. It's in one of those gated communities where even the security guards look like they've completed an MBA. The lawns are so manicured they make you question your life choices, and the villas look like they were designed by someone who's allergic to the concept of "too much."

As I step out of the car and take in the opulent surroundings, I can't help but think: Gurgaon isn't just trying to prove it's arrived. It's throwing a party, sending out embossed invitations, and making sure the guest list only includes people who can afford to RSVP.

Food: When Dining Becomes a Competitive Sport

If Gurgaon's food scene were a person, it'd be that Instagram influencer who claims they "live to eat" but never forgets to hashtag their smoothie bowl #cleanliving. Driving into Gurgaon is like crossing an invisible barrier where food stops being about sustenance and becomes an Olympic event for the taste buds. Everything here is plated like it's about to audition for Master Chef.

We roll up to Cyber Hub, Gurgaon's answer to "What if a food court took steroids and joined a luxury gym?" The restaurants are sleek, glass-clad temples of gastronomy where each plate looks like it should come with an artist's statement. Forget eating—you're here to curate your culinary narrative. Take the sushi place, for instance. It's not just sushi; it's an experience. Each roll is topped with edible gold flakes, because why not, and the soy sauce probably has a PhD. This isn't food for hungry people. This is food for people who want to look deep in thought while discussing "umami profiles."

We eventually settle on a swanky Italian spot, the kind that tries to make you feel like you're dining in Tuscany, even though you're technically next to a skyscraper named "Millennium Tower Phase II." The menu reads like a love letter to food snobs—truffle pasta, saffron risotto, pizza with burrata flown in from a goat named Luigi. Don't get me wrong, the food is delicious, but there's something hilariously over-the-top about it. It's like the chefs are competing to see who can make you feel the most unworthy of their creations.

As we eat, the conversations around us are just as rich as the food. I catch snippets about angel investors, boutique vineyards, and someone's trip to the Maldives where they "discovered themselves." No one's talking about the food. Because in Gurgaon, eating isn't about flavors; it's about flexing. Your meal isn't complete unless someone across the room envies your table.

By the time dessert rolls around—some deconstructed tiramisu that looks like modern art—I'm already half-expecting the waiter to deliver a motivational speech about success with the check.

As we leave the restaurant and step back into the meticulously planned streets, I glance back at Cyber Hub, glowing like a jewel in the night. It's impressive, no doubt.

But honestly speaking, Gurgaon unnecessarily pretends to be something it is not.

Shopping: Olympics of Luxury Retail

Shopping in Gurgaon isn't just an activity; it's a sport—and not the kind where you casually stroll into a store for a packet of chips. No, this is the Olympics of luxury retail, where your wallet is the torchbearer and only the fittest bank account survives.

Driving toward one of Gurgaon's opulent malls feels like entering the arena. The buildings practically dare you to outspend the person walking ten feet ahead of you. It greets you like a modern-day Versailles: polished marble floors that look like they're allergic to dirt, chandeliers that belong in royal ballrooms, and ceilings so high you're convinced they might brush against heaven. Even the valet parking has a swagger, as if to remind you that your car—no matter how shiny—is probably the least expensive thing within a two-mile radius.

Inside, the ambiance is a mix of theatre and power play. Escalators whisk you upward, but let's be honest—this isn't just about convenience. It's an unspoken hierarchy, a literal climb to higher levels of luxury. Each floor is like its own kingdom: couture on one, gadgets on another, and somewhere in between, a food court that feels more like a Michelin-starred convention than a place to grab fries. The designer boutiques are basically temples. And the mannequins? They're not just wearing clothes—they're serving looks. The garments shimmer so intensely under the strategically placed lights that you half expect them to hum with divine power.

Enter Chanel, Gucci, or Louis Vuitton, and the sales associates greet you with the kind of practiced enthusiasm that says, "We know you're not buying, but we'll humor you." They offer champagne or macarons—because apparently, browsing requires hydration and snacks of a certain caliber. It's not just shopping; it's like starring in your own reality show where every purchase is a plot twist. You don't buy a bag here. You "invest in an heirloom," as the salesperson whispers with the gravitas of a Netflix narrator.

Downstairs, the electronics section is its own spectacle. Smartphones and tablets are displayed like ancient artifacts in glass cases, surrounded by lighting so soft and flattering it could make your phone's cracked screen look couture. The staff are less salespeople and more evangelists. They speak of megapixels and RAM with the kind of reverence usually reserved for poetry. And let's not forget the smart appliances. Refrigerators with touchscreens and coffee machines that know your mood based on your sigh? They don't just promise efficiency—they promise enlightenment. Forget "functionality"; it's all about how your toaster reflects your personality.

The food courts in Gurgaon are extra. You won't find your usual fast-food suspects here; instead, it's a global gastronomic parade. Chefs sculpt sushi rolls like edible masterpieces, and pizzas emerge from ovens with crusts so golden they'd make Midas jealous. You're handed your meal on plates so fancy, you feel a little guilty eating off them. The kicker? No one in these food courts actually looks hungry. They're too busy photographing their meals, angling their cameras just right to capture the artisanal steam wafting off their coffee. Eating here isn't about filling your stomach; it's about filling your Instagram feed.

But let's not kid ourselves—this is Gurgaon. The whole shopping experience is less about finding joy in a good deal and more about playing your part in a choreographed performance of wealth. Each store, each interaction, each bite of overpriced gelato is designed to remind you that you're participating in something exclusive.

And yet, beneath the polished marble and curated displays, there's a certain absurdity to it all. The perfection is almost too perfect, like a movie set where the walls are just cardboard props. It's hard to shake the feeling that the grandeur is a bit...hollow.

As you leave the mall, weighed down by bags and existential musings, the Gurgaon skyline twinkles in the evening light, as if winking at your drained wallet. It's an experience, no doubt—a glittering carnival of capitalism that's equal parts dazzling and exhausting.

In Gurgaon, shopping isn't just a pastime. It's a production, a spectacle, a quest to remind you that luxury isn't just a choice—it's a lifestyle. And while it's undeniably impressive, sometimes you just want to buy a T-shirt without being offered champagne!

Festival Frenzy: Diwali in Gurgaon

Diwali (Hindu festival of lights) in Gurgaon is like a stage production where everyone is trying to win "Best Supporting Actor", but no one can stop flashing their diamond-studded accessories. It's as though the city said, "Let's make this a contest for who can turn their home into a Bollywood music video." The streets are glittering with enough lights to rival Las Vegas on New Year's Eve. Seriously, if you threw a 3D pair of glasses on and looked out the window, you might think you're in a Pixar movie.

Even the air seems to sparkle, as if someone decided that air pollution just wasn't flashy enough.

But this time, I decided to escape the glamour overload. Instead of getting blinded by the twinkling lights and those ridiculously overpriced firecrackers that only go off after you've gotten comfortable on the couch, I decided to experience *Diwali* the way it was meant to be: no fireworks, no neon laser shows, and definitely no six-hour traffic jams. I found myself at my friend's house, where the *Diwali* vibes were more about connection and less about flexing your latest iPhone model.

The house had this quiet, understated charm, like the "artsy" Instagram influencer who doesn't even try to look perfect. There were candles flickering like they were on the cover of a "How To Be Zen" book, and the whole place smelled like sweet *gulab jamuns* (a popular milk-solid-based sweet, consisting of fried dough balls soaked in rose-scented sugar syrup), as if the gods themselves had decided to descend and hand them out as a peace offering.

There were marigold flowers everywhere—more marigolds than the average Indian wedding. But it was calm, inviting, and not an inch of it screamed, "We spent 50,000 rupees on this." And then, the shocker: there were NO FIREWORKS. Yup, I said it. For a moment, I thought I'd wandered into an alternate universe where *Diwali* is about actually enjoying the festival rather than making your pets think the world is ending. Instead, there were sparklers—glittering but safe— and no one was trying to create the biggest, loudest explosion that would make even the neighbors from two streets down call in a noise complaint. It was refreshing, like drinking water after a month of soda.

The family's reason for the quiet, environmentally-friendly celebration was something I respected deeply. They were adamant about not contributing to the pollution and chaos that so often accompanies the festival. They explained it like they were giving me a TED Talk, but with the added bonus of *laddoos* (Indian round shaped sweet) and *samosas* (a deep friend triangular savory snack containing spiced vegetables). "Fireworks? No, thank you. We'd rather have clean air," they said.

Honestly, I almost wanted to apologize for every firecracker I'd ever lit in my life.

As the night wore on, I realized that this decision, though seemingly minor, really made me rethink the nature of *Diwali*. Here, it was about family, food, and honoring the spirit of the festival without trying to burn down the atmosphere—literally. It was a reminder that *Diwali* didn't need to be about impressing the neighbors with your firepower. Instead, it was about spreading light, love, and perhaps, just a little less noise.

This was the Diwali I'll tell my grandchildren about. And it'll involve no medical bills for firecracker injuries.

The Glitterati: People of Gurgaon

Gurgaon is where the rich and famous come to flex—and by "flex," I mean they're actually bending their luxury cars into contorted shapes to show how much money they can throw away. It's like the city is one big "Who Can Buy The Most Expensive Thing" contest, and everyone is convinced they're winning.

In the distance, you can almost hear the sound of an ATM coughing up cash like it's allergic to money. The elites of Gurgaon are a breed of their own, living in buildings so tall they make you question if gravity is even real. You'll find them in penthouses that scream, "I could probably see my house from here, but let's be real, I don't even need to look that far." Their homes are furnished with more designer brands than a Paris Fashion Week runway. You'd think the place was a showroom for things rich people actually need. They have smart fridges that probably tell them their life choices are unhealthy, but the fridge itself is probably too busy calculating the value of its contents and saying, "Did you really need that avocado toast, sir?"

And don't get me started on the high-powered executive who lives in this "perfection" bubble. His office desk is probably made of the rarest wood in the world (and also, probably, in the process of becoming extinct). He's the kind of guy who makes the rest of us feel like our lives are stuck on "pause," while his are on "super-speed mode." Meanwhile, his penthouse is like a luxurious jail cell—beautiful, but really lonely. He probably spends more time adjusting his tie than actually living, yet, ironically, his greatest wish is to spend a weekend doing absolutely nothing but binge-watching Netflix. It's like the Truman Show, but without the cameras.

Then there's the socialite, who's basically living a life you've only seen in Instagram stories. They've got the perfect angles, the perfect lighting, and the perfect filter. Seriously, I don't know if I should be jealous of their life or just be worried about how much Photoshop is involved. To her followers, she's the ultimate influencer—living a dream life where even the traffic is made of rainbows and unicorns. But when the lights go out and she's alone, she's just like us: wondering if that cupcake is going to solve her existential crisis. Newsflash: it won't. But it will make her feel better for about 30 minutes.

Meanwhile, the young startup moguls are living their lives like caffeinated squirrels. They're trying to change the world, one pitch deck at a time. But the truth is, their startup culture is built on the power of 8 hours of sleep a month, infinite cups of coffee, and hoping that their Wi-Fi holds up during a pitch. It's a business plan based on the idea that if you tell people you're innovating, they'll just give you money. They're constantly hustling, networking, and trying to raise capital, but I don't think anyone has told them that sleep is a necessary biological function. Seriously, they're one caffeine-induced panic attack away from posting a "Help, I'm drowning in meetings" tweet.

In the less glamorous corners of Gurgaon, the working class is just trying to survive without any glamour attached. They're the real MVPs, making sure that everyone else can keep pretending their luxury lives are as flawless as their Instagram posts. These are the folks who take care of the real grunt work—like cleaning up after the party ends or making sure the pizza arrives on time. It's like they're the background actors in a movie about a city that doesn't even know they exist. Honestly, I can't even imagine what it's like to live in a city where your job is to just exist while everyone else tries to figure out what's for dinner. It's like a survival show, but with fewer fire challenges and more spreadsheets.

If Gurgaon were a person...

If Gurgaon were a person, it would be the quintessential embodiment of a self-assured celebrity, striding through life with an air of effortless charisma and an unshakable sense of grandeur.

Picture this persona stepping out of a state-of-the-art luxury vehicle, dressed in an impeccably tailored suit that radiates not just style but an almost palpable aura of success. Their very presence is a carefully crafted performance, designed to dazzle and dominate, each moment a calculated display of elegance and power. This celebrity doesn't merely exist; they command the world around them. Their life is a continuous showcase of opulence and influence.

Imagine their residence: a penthouse apartment perched high above the city, offering sweeping vistas that stretch as far as the eye can see. The interior is a testament to an uncompromising pursuit of perfection—glossy marble floors, bespoke furniture, and walls adorned with rare art pieces. It's a space where every detail, from the precision of the lighting to the arrangement of the décor, serves to reinforce their status as the pinnacle of sophistication.

The celebrity's social calendar is nothing short of a whirlwind of high-profile events. From exclusive charity galas to fashion shows that set the trends for the season, every event is an opportunity for them to shine. Their arrival at these gatherings is met with a flurry of attention, as cameras flash and whispers ripple through the crowd. They are the centerpiece of every gathering, their opinions and actions scrutinized and celebrated in equal measure. The media buzzes with their every move, elevating their status to that of an almost mythic figure.

But beneath this veneer of supreme confidence and constant acclaim lies a more nuanced reality. The celebrity's public image, while seemingly flawless, is a carefully maintained facade. The pressure to sustain this level of success is immense and relentless. Each accolade is not just a personal triumph but a marker of the constant need to outdo oneself and others. The applause and admiration, though gratifying, are fleeting, and the fear of falling from grace looms ever-present.

In private, the celebrity grapples with the weight of their public persona. The carefully curated image can feel like a gilded cage, where the demands of maintaining perfection overshadow the pursuit of genuine happiness. Their interactions are often a balancing act of charm and diplomacy, designed to ensure they remain at the forefront of social and professional circles. The constant need to be admired and envied can create a profound sense of isolation, where the very success that defines them also isolates them from authentic connections.

The life of this celebrity is a high-wire act of grandeur and vulnerability. They live in a world where every success is celebrated, but each moment of triumph is quickly overshadowed by the need for the next. The public's adoration, while exhilarating, is matched by an equal measure of anxiety—an ever- present fear of losing their exalted position. The constant pressure to maintain an image of perfection can be as exhausting as it is exhilarating, a cycle of achievement and expectation that defines their existence.

As they move through their days, the celebrity embodies the paradoxes of their world: a dazzling spectacle of success and opulence juxtaposed with the internal struggle of keeping up appearances. They are a figure who commands respect and admiration, yet behind the polished surface lies the reality of living under the unrelenting gaze of both public and private scrutiny.

Thus, if Gurgaon were a person, it would be this self-assured celebrity—a figure who represents the zenith of success and luxury while also navigating the complex and often hidden challenges of sustaining such a position. This celebrity's life is a reflection of the paradoxes inherent in a world of dazzling achievement, where the pursuit of perfection is both a source of immense satisfaction and a profound challenge. Their existence is a testament to the heights of success and the subtle unseen struggles of maintaining an impeccable image in the relentless glare of the public eye.

The Great Escape: Leaving Gurgaon

Leaving Gurgaon feels like walking out of a VIP section and back into reality—like you've been living in a very exclusive club, and then someone finally says, "Okay, you've had your fill. Time to go back to the regular world where no one is showing off their latest diamond-studded phone case." The contrast is so real that you can almost hear the whoosh as the city's ostentatious glitter fades into a soft, forgiving blur.

As you drive out, the roads go from pristine, luxury-laden highways to the kind of places where cows still consider themselves the traffic controllers. The high rises that seemed so imposing start to feel like distant memories—like that one night in the club that you tried to pretend was way more fun than it actually was. And instead of smooth roads lined with gleaming malls, you find yourself in areas where potholes are more frequent than Uber drivers. Welcome to the world of "No-one's-watching-now." But there's a certain comfort in it. It's like stepping off a treadmill and realizing that walking is just fine.

You leave behind the buzz of Gurgaon's high-energy, high-anxiety atmosphere and enter a more relaxed, real-world vibe. The sky opens up, the air smells a little more... earthy, and suddenly, you realize that people don't live their lives with a stopwatch ticking every five seconds. There's space for conversation, breathing, and not checking your bank account every ten minutes to make sure you're still doing okay.

As you get further away, you can't help but notice how the landscape shifts—glistening shopping malls turn into green fields, the concrete jungle transforms into rustic simplicity, and people are no longer afraid to make eye contact for fear of being judged on their choice of shoes. It's like entering a place where everything slows down, and you start realizing that you never really needed that new iPhone to be happy. You can actually just sit back, relax, and breathe, without constantly wondering how you compare to everyone else on social media.

What do I carry from Gurgaon?

Looking at Gurgaon, I can't help but think about the stark contrast between its glittering façade and the hidden struggles beneath. Behind the polished facades of luxury apartments and sleek cars, there's a constant push to maintain a life of perfection, often at the cost of inner peace and genuine connection.

This complex dynamic shaped me in unexpected ways. Gurgaon has opened my eyes to the fragility of external appearances. I learned that wealth, though powerful, can often feel isolating—like a barrier that keeps people distant from what truly matters. The pressure to meet high expectations taught me about the dangers of defining success by material standards alone. I came to understand that while ambition is important, it can't be the sole measure of one's worth.

In Gurgaon, I saw that fulfillment doesn't lie in the accumulation of things, but in the quality of our connections and the ability to find balance between outward success and inner peace. This realization has shaped my own journey, reminding me that I don't need to chase the glitz and glamour of the city's exterior to feel valuable.

Darbhanga: The Cultural Capital of Bihar

Darbhanga is a historic city in Bihar, India, known for its rich cultural heritage and as a prominent center of the Mithila region. Often referred to as the "Cultural Capital of Bihar," it is famous for the Mithila painting tradition, classical music, and its royal lineage under the Darbhanga Raj. The city houses the iconic Darbhanga Fort, the majestic Raj Darbhanga Palace, and sacred ponds that enhance its old-world charm. Darbhanga is also an educational hub, hosting Lalit Narayan Mithila University. It serves as a gateway to exploring Mithilanchal's vibrant traditions including its unique art called *Madhubani* (named after a city in Bihar), folk arts, and cuisine.

From Plane to Panic: A Darbhanga Survival Guide

Stepping off the plane at Darbhanga Airport felt like being swallowed by a living beast. The heat hit me first, a wet blanket of humidity that instantly made my clothes stick to my skin. It was like the air itself had conspired to turn me into soggy bread. The airport terminal was a dense, buzzing hive of activity, and I was the confused bee wondering how I ended up there. People were everywhere, moving with a kind of organized chaos that defied easy understanding. Women in vibrant sarees and men in dhotis filled every available space, their clothes a kaleidoscope of colors that seemed almost too bright under the harsh fluorescent lights. Children darted through the crowd like fish in a river, giggling and shrieking with the boundless energy of little humans who probably hadn't been on a plane for five hours straight with a middle seat.

The voices in *Maithili* (local language here) were a loud, unending melody of guttural consonants and rolling vowels, colliding with each other like bumper cars. It was the kind of soundtrack that made you want subtitles for real life. Every conversation was a battle of volume, like a competition to see who could out-shout the airport's announcements.

The floor beneath my feet was uneven, worn smooth in places by countless feet, yet still gritty with dust and the occasional sticky mystery patch. Every step felt like an adventure—one wrong move and you might slide into an unintended split. Navigating the crowd was like playing an impromptu game of human Tetris. People pressed in on all sides, the brush of fabric, the jostling shoulders, the occasional whiff of too much *attar* (perfume oil)—it was an immersive experience.

The air was thick with the smells of sweat, diesel, and the unmistakable aroma of deep-fried street food lurking somewhere nearby, tempting and slightly concerning. Finally, we slid into the beaten seats of our beige Maruti

Suzuki car, which welcomed us back like an old, slightly musty friend. The car's interior clung to the smell of old leather, faint traces of past journeys, and a hint of something that might've been spilled *chai* (milktea) from five years ago. The engine roared—or rather wheezed—to life with a sound that could've been a sigh of resignation.

Leaving the chaotic din of Darbhanga Airport, the Maruti jolted over the uneven terrain, each bump reminding us that the car's suspension had probably retired before we were born. The roads were alive with market stalls bursting with fruits, vendors hollering prices, and a honking orchestra of rickshaws, scooters, and pedestrians who believed traffic rules were merely suggestions. We bounced and swayed over potholes that seemed less like cracks in the road and more like portals to another dimension. Every jolt made the car creak ominously, as if it were whispering, "Please retire me."

As we neared *Nani's* (maternal grandmother) house, the scenery shifted to open fields and thatched-roof houses. The ancient banyan tree at the crossroads looked like it had seen every argument and gossip session in the village, its roots stretching out as if it wanted to eavesdrop some more. Finally, *Nani's* house came into view, standing solid and proud by the pond. The Maruti gave one final shudder as we parked, as if to say, "Thank goodness that's over."

We stepped out, the pond glinting in the sunlight, while I swore I saw a frog give me a side-eye for disturbing its peace. Inside *Nani's* house, the air was heavy with a silence that felt like it had been collecting dust for years. Dust particles floated lazily in the sunlight streaming through the windows, like they were auditioning for a slow-motion music video. And there it was: the infamous trunk in the corner of the room, the one that haunted my childhood dreams. I remembered that fat grey moth that flew out of it when I was little, a creature so villainous it might as well have been a mini-Dracula. I could still hear Nani's uncontrollable laughter after my dramatic escape—her tears of amusement as I lay sprawled in the hallway, convinced that the moth had cursed me. Looking back now, it was hard to see that trunk as anything more than an old box full of boring papers. But for the sake of my childhood honor, I decided to glare at it anyway, just in case another moth was lying in wait.

A Flavorful Journey Through Darbhanga's Culinary Magic

The musty smell faded, replaced by something far more primal—smoke, spice, and the unmistakable scent of fish cooking over an open flame. If air fresheners ever tried to bottle it, they'd probably call it "Rural BBQ: Burnt Dreams Edition." My mind drifted to those long, sticky evenings in Darbhanga, where the heat felt like it was trying to smother us, but the laughter pulled us through. Those evenings revolved around food—not just any food, but proper Maithili meals that could knock out a heavyweight.

Rice was the star of the plate, accompanied by *daal* (a dish made with lentils or other split pulses), spiced fresh water fish, and tangy yoghurt. Vegetables got their moment too, seasoned so well you almost forgot they were healthy. And then came the sweets. Oh, the sweets. *Pua* (fried fritters soaked in jaggery syrup) and *kheer* (creamy rice pudding) were the finishing move, leaving you full, happy, and ready to crash for a solid afternoon nap.

In the middle of it all was *Nani,* the kitchen's undisputed MVP (Most Valuable Player). Her cooking wasn't about recipes; it was instinct. She'd toss in a pinch of this, a handful of that, and somehow everything came out perfect! Watching her cook was mesmerizing—chopping, stirring, tasting, and scolding someone all at once. It felt like magic, except you could eat it.

Family dinners around the fire weren't just about the food, though. They were about chaos, jokes, and the kind of laughter that made you choke on your rice if you weren't careful. Like the time I begged to try flipping the fish on the skewer, only to send it tumbling into the fire in a dramatic sizzle. I braced for *Nani's* disappointment, but instead, everyone burst into laughter—even her. That charred fish, which probably should've been left in the flames, somehow became "the best fish we've ever had," thanks to her diplomatic declaration.

Looking back, these meals weren't just food; they were a connection. Eating *Nani's* food with the whole family felt like plugging into something bigger—a tradition, a culture, a shared history. It was comforting, even when life outside felt uncertain. Now, when I think of those meals, I don't just remember the taste of smoky fish or sweet *pua.* I remember what it meant to be together, to laugh at my clumsiness, and to feel at home. And somehow, that memory always brings a little joy, even on the gloomiest of days.

Bargaining Bootcamp: The Darbhanga Way

I heard it—a soft creak in the doorway, as familiar as the sound of my own breathing. No need to look; it was my *Nanu* (maternal grandfather). His footsteps always had a rhythm, slow and steady, like he had all the time in the world.

"You ready?" He asked, his voice rough but warm, like sandpaper with a soft spot. He stood in the doorway, tall and broad, filling the space like he owned it. His face was a roadmap of wrinkles, softened by the faintest smile, and his eyes carried that mischievous spark, the kind that said he wasn't done surprising the world.

"We're going to Tower Chowk," he declared, almost daring the Universe to say no. "Can't let those vendors think they've got the upper hand, can we?" He laughed, a deep rumble that felt like it could shake the walls. Following *Nanu* out of the house always felt like stepping into his domain. The city of Darbhanga matched his energy—loud, chaotic, and absolutely unbothered by what anyone else thought. Tower Chowk wasn't just a market; it was his stage. Every vendor, stray dog, and rickshaw puller seemed to know him. If there was a secret handshake of small-town royalty, *Nanu* had mastered it.

The market hit all your senses at once: the smell of *samosas* frying in oil, the tangy spice of *chaat masala* (a type of spice mixture), the sweet pull of *jalebis* (an Indian sweet made of a coil of deep-fried batter that is soaked briefly in sugar syrup), and the constant noise of a city that never learned about volume control. Walking through it with *Nanu* was like being in a parade where he was the main float. He moved slowly, deliberately, while I was busy dodging potholes like a contestant on a game show. At the sweet shop, he ordered a box of *laddoos* with the kind of authority that made the shopkeeper snap to attention. "Don't eat them all before we get home," he said, handing them over with a wink. Spoiler alert: one didn't survive the walk.

Then there was the fish market—chaotic, smelly, and somehow *Nanu's* favorite spot. He inspected the *rohu* fish like a jeweler examining diamonds, while the fishmonger muttered something about him being the Sherlock Holmes of seafood. I found myself reading the headlines on the newspaper wrapping, one of which involved a goat attending a wedding. Darbhanga news was never boring.

As we left Tower Chowk, the sun was setting, painting the market in softer colors. The chaos mellowed, and for a moment, the city felt peaceful. I looked at *Nanu*, his face glowing in the golden light, and thought about how the city and he were cut from the same cloth—resilient, a little rough, but always full of life.

Back home, the fish would cook over the fire, and *Nanu's* stories would fill the air. The day wasn't just about errands; it was about the unspoken lessons he passed on—how to face the world with humor and grit. If Tower Chowk was the city's heart, *Nanu* was the beat that kept it alive.

Darbhanga's Colorful Cast: A Portrait of its People

The people of Darbhanga carry a weight with them, something almost palpable in the air, like the thick humidity that clings to your skin and never quite lets go. And by "weight," I don't just mean their existential burdens—half the population walks around carrying sacks of rice, pots of milk, or, in one particularly memorable instance, a live chicken under one arm and a basket of mangoes on their head. There's a darkness in their eyes, a shadow that lingers just beneath the surface, born of years spent fighting battles most of the world doesn't even know exist—like wrestling with the *tehsildar* (land revenue officer) over land records that seem to have been written by someone with a grudge against coherent penmanship.

Life here isn't just a daily grind; it's a constant struggle, a war of attrition against forces that seem insurmountable—poverty, corruption, and cows with absolutely no respect for road safety. And yet, they endure. And aspire. The men walk with a certain heaviness, their shoulders hunched, not just from the weight of the day's labor but from the unseen burdens they carry—like their mother-in-law's opinions, which, as any married man in Darbhanga will tell you, are heavier than a tractor. Their faces are weathered, cracked like the dry earth they till, each line a testament to a lifetime of hard truths and missed cricket matches thanks to power cuts. There's a coldness in their demeanor, a hardness that speaks of trust betrayed too many times, of dreams deferred until they crumbled to dust—or, more accurately, were stolen by their neighbor's nephew, who somehow got a "government job" they'd been eyeing since 2004. They don't smile easily; when they do, it's often tinged with irony or the bitter aftertaste of reality—or maybe it's just the *paan* (betel leaves and nuts) that stains their teeth a violent red, making every grin look vaguely homicidal.

The women, for all their grace, hold a quiet ferocity. Their beauty is fierce, like a storm on the horizon—something you can admire from a distance but would do well to fear up close. They've had to be strong, stronger than the men sometimes, because the world demands it—and also because someone has to chase the aforementioned cows off the front yard. They bear the brunt of life's cruelties with a silent rage, their eyes hard as steel, their hands rough from years of toil and disciplining children with a single look so powerful it could curdle milk. Their love is not just soft or tender; it's a protective shield, forged in the fires of survival. It's the kind of love that doesn't coddle but makes sure you're fed, even if it's with *lauki sabzi* (bottle gourd dish cooked with spices), which no one asked for but everyone eats because you don't mess with Maa. When they speak, their words cut through the air like a knife, sharp and precise, leaving no room for misunderstanding—or arguments, because anyone who's tried knows that debating a Darbhanga woman is like arguing with gravity: pointless and guaranteed to end with you on the floor.

The children in Darbhanga aren't the innocent, carefree souls you'd expect. They grow up fast here, too fast, learning the rules of a harsh world long before they should—like how to dodge the local *mukhiya's* (local chief) dog or haggle with the *sabziwala* (vegetable vendor) for an extra potato. Their games have an edge to them, a reflection of the reality they see around them every day—whether it's cricket with a deflated ball or the classic "who can climb the mango tree fastest without getting caught by the angry landlord." There's a certain look in their eyes, a wariness that shouldn't belong to someone so young, as if they already know that Santa isn't coming because the postmaster *babu* never delivered their letter. Their laughter is loud, but there's a hollowness to it, a recognition that joy is fleeting, and the world is always waiting to snatch it away—usually in the form of a shouting uncle who doesn't appreciate a makeshift cricket pitch in front of his gate. And yet, there's resilience; these kids could probably survive a zombie apocalypse armed with nothing but a *lattu* (spinning top) and sheer audacity.

And then there are the elders—the ones who've seen it all, who've watched the world change and stayed exactly the same, mostly because change requires paperwork, and paperwork in Darbhanga is a labyrinth no one dares to enter. They sit in the shade, their eyes clouded with memories that no one else could understand, stories that are too heavy to share—or maybe they just enjoy watching the young ones struggle to figure out life while muttering, *"Hamare zamane mein…"* (During our times). They speak in riddles and proverbs, their words laced with the bitterness of a life that never gave them what they deserved, like the time they missed a *Ramleela* (dramatic performance of the Hindu epic Ramayana) because their buffalo decided to go rogue. They've outlived their dreams, survived long enough to see the next generation repeat their mistakes—sometimes in the exact same ways, like marrying into families with even more chaotic servants. Their wisdom is tinged with cynicism, their advice as harsh as the reality they know too well, and yet somehow, they always have time to yell at kids for running too loudly near their *charpai* (cot).

Darbhanga's people are survivors, but there's a cost to that survival. It's in the way they move, the way they talk, the way they look at you with eyes that have seen too much—and yet still notice when you're not wearing slippers, which they will comment on, loudly. They are strong, but it's a strength born of necessity, not choice. They don't just hope for a better life because just hoping is a luxury they can't afford—they aspire and slog for it, even when their last attempt at hope was dashed when the new bridge project turned into a "bridge to nowhere" thanks to the contractor's *chacha* (uncle) pocketing the funds. They focus on getting through today, on making it till tomorrow, and that's enough. There's darkness here, a shadow that hangs over everything, but there is always light at the end of the tunnel. It's part of the people, part of the land, woven into the very fabric of Darbhanga. And in that darkness, there's a kind of beauty—a raw, unfiltered truth that strips away all pretenses and leaves you with the stark reality of life. It's harsh, it's unforgiving, but it's real. And in a world full of illusions, there's something almost comforting about that. Plus, where else would you get to witness an argument between two uncles about whose *paan ki dukaan* (betel leaves shop) sells the best *zarda* (flavored tobacco)?

If Darbhanga were a person...

It would be a middle-aged man with a sharp gaze and a face lined from years of getting by. His skin would be sun-beaten and rough, his clothes simple—probably a *kurta* (a long, loose shirt which usually reaches knee height) that had seen better days and sandals hanging on for dear life. He'd move with purpose, navigating chaos like it was second nature, sidestepping potholes and dodging life's curveballs without breaking stride. His voice would be straightforward, with a dry wit that could cut you down or crack you up, depending on his mood. He'd smell of *chai* (milktea), fried snacks, and a hint of smoke, like a blend of everything happening in the streets around him. He wouldn't waste time with pretense—he'd tell it like it is, whether you wanted to hear it or not. But under all that practicality and sarcasm, there'd be depth—a quiet resilience that came from years of making do and moving forward.

Farewell to Chaos: A Darbhanga Goodbye

Leaving Darbhanga would feel like leaving behind that one friend who knows all your secrets, the good and the bad.

As the landscape blurred past, I thought about the men who would still be sitting at those *chai* stalls, their voices rising and falling like the smoke from their cigarettes, each puff filled with equal parts philosophy and gossip about whose buffalo had wandered into whose field. They were experts in *chai*-fueled problem-solving, which mostly involved heated debates that solved nothing but somehow made everyone feel better.

I thought about the women who would continue their endless cycle of work, their hands never stopping, not even when the weight of the world—or their mother-in-law's endless sarcastic remarks—bore down on their shoulders. These were women who could cook a full meal, fix a torn sari, and break up a neighborhood fight with just one sharp look. Honestly, they were so efficient, I wouldn't have been surprised if they could churn butter, braid a child's hair, and scold their husbands all at the same time.

I thought about the children, their laughter echoing through the narrow lanes, a fleeting sound that would be swallowed up by the noise of the city, or by the occasional goat that decided it was auditioning for Indian Idol. These kids weren't just playing games; they were basically running full-scale neighborhood startups, with one selling marbles, another renting out a cricket bat, and the smallest one acting as security enforcement in exchange for a half-eaten biscuit. I'm pretty sure some of them had more business acumen than half the MBA grads in Delhi.

Last but not the least, I thought about the elders, sitting in their quiet corners, watching as the world changed and stayed the same, their eyes heavy with the knowledge of all that had been lost and all that would never be—and also with the knowledge of exactly who in the family hadn't returned their last loan. These were people who could turn a single proverb into a three-hour sermon, complete with side stories, unsolicited advice, and the occasional curse word slipped in for dramatic effect. Their wisdom was unparalleled, but their sarcasm? Deadlier than the chilies they grew in their backyard.

As I was leaving Darbhanga behind, I realized that I wasn't just leaving Darbhanga— I was carrying it with me - the darkness, the resilience, the rawness of that place—it was all inside of me, like an annoying but oddly comforting neighbor who always shows up uninvited but never leaves you feeling alone. I wasn't able to shake it off even if I tried. It stayed with me in the manner in which I handled crowds, in my no-nonsense attitude, in the way I appreciated the little things. The spirit of Darbhanga tagged along with me, long after I had left that place, which made me feel invincible—or at least, too stubborn to quit.

What do I carry from Darbhanga?

The people of Darbhanga, with their hard faces and harder lives, have shaped me in profound ways. They were the ones who taught me that life wasn't kind, that you had to take what you could and hold on to it with both hands, preferably while side-eyeing anyone who even thought about asking for a share. After all, if life wasn't going to be generous, why should they be? They were the ones who showed me that strength wasn't about muscles or bravado, but about surviving in a world that didn't care whether you lived or died—and often seemed actively rooting for the latter.

In Darbhanga, every day was a test of patience, resourcefulness, and your ability to find humor in things like electricity cuts during peak summer or the neighbor's goat stealing your laundry.

There was no room for illusions, no place for the softness of dreams, unless your dream involved negotiating with the neighborhood cow to stop blocking the main road. There was only the hard, unyielding reality of survival—of making it through one day so you could face the next, armed with *chai*, a rusty bicycle, and a stubbornness that could put even the monsoon rains to shame. And this side of reality has become a part of me; a shadow that I know follows me no matter where I go.

Darbhanga, is where the deep-rooted traditions of my family come to life. It carries more than just history—it holds the essence of personal connections, family, and the stories passed down through generations. Every corner, every street, has layers of meaning, and these spaces are where I find my roots. It is more than just location to me; it is where my mother's past takes root, reminding me that every place we come from shapes who we are.

Visiting my *Nani's* house near the pond allowed me to experience the timeless rituals and connections that define my maternal side. It is a place where tradition holds its ground. I understood that being grounded in tradition doesn't mean being stuck in time; instead, it gives us the roots to grow, evolve, and find our place in the world.

I didn't live there, but the few times I visited left a lasting impact on me. The festivals, the shared meals, the quiet mornings by the pond—each of these experiences taught me the power of continuity, of belonging to a community that values the past as much as the present.

It was in Darbhanga that I learned the strength of family ties, how stories are passed from one generation to the next not just through words, but through actions, traditions, and unspoken bonds.

Bokaro: A City of Steel and Determination

Bokaro is a city that holds deep personal significance for me because it's my dad's hometown. He grew up there; his family's historical roots run deep in this city. Even today, the stories of my dad's childhood linger in our conversations.

Nestled in the state of Jharkhand, in Eastern India, it's also known as "Bokaro Steel City", due to its steel industry, particularly the Bokaro Steel Plant (BSP), one of the largest in Asia.

The city signifies how India started rebuilding itself after colonial rule w.r.t industrialization and township.

Trainwreck Arrival:

The train screeched to a halt, jolting me out of my half-asleep, half-annoyed stupor, and signaling our arrival. We stepped out of our cramped cubicle, only to be greeted by the collective perfume of sweat and stress. It's like everyone on that train had been marinating in their own anxiety, and now we were all sous chefs in some unholy kitchen.

As I surveyed the chaotic crowd, I couldn't help but marvel at how quickly we'd all devolved into animals—pushing, shoving, and snarling to claim a few inches of space. And, of course, I was right there with them, elbows out, channeling my inner linebacker to reach the door. Was I proud of it? No. Did I have a choice? No again! After what felt like a wrestling match with strangers, I made it to the door, yanked the luggage, and stumbled out of the train like I'd just escaped a hostage situation. My paranoia had me convinced that someone was going to push me out onto the tracks as karmic retribution, but the cold Bokaro air hit me before anyone else could, sending shivers down my spine and a clear message: Welcome to Bokaro, home of bad but clean railway station design and good memories.

Then came the stairs—those wretched, unholy stairs. Climb up, climb down—it's like the railway station was designed by someone who had a personal vendetta against travelers. By the time we reached the parking lot, my arms were protesting louder than a toddler denied a lollipop. But there it was, waiting for us like a loyal friend: the fiery red Maruti Suzuki car. It's practically family at this point, with how often it's been our chariot of escape.

As we drove through Bokaro's streets, I felt the tug of nostalgia pulling me in every direction. Every landmark had a story, and every story had dad at the center of it. There was the Jawaharlal Nehru Biological Park, which Dad insisted was the town's pride, though I'm pretty sure its main residents are pigeons and boredom. Then there was Delhi Public School (DPS) Bokaro, where Dad spent his youth earning the title of "kid-gangster." I still can't imagine him as anything but the slightly grumpy, extremely dad-like figure he is now, but hey, everyone's got a past.

By the time we pulled into the driveway, I was running on fumes but ready for the final boss battle: Coco. That dog greets me like I'm a soldier returning from war, all wagging tail and unrestrained excitement. It's like being tackled by joy itself.

Inside, the familiar smells of home hit me—curry, old wood, and something that's probably incense but could just as easily be mothballs. My aunt was waiting, armed with her signature "you're too skinny" hug, which I've learned to accept as a tradition rather than an observation.

After scrubbing the train germs off me, I joined the family on the couch. This was prime tea time, a sacred ritual of laughter, stories, and snacks. For a little while, we were free from responsibilities—no work for dad, no errands for mom, no academic pressure for me, and no mischief for my brother (though that part was temporary, I'm sure).

Even the *samosas* (a deep friend triangular savory snack containing spiced vegetables) seemed to taste better in Bokaro, like they'd been fried in pure nostalgia. As tea time wound down, my aunt and I planned our outing to City Center. She humored my snack obsession, though I knew she was probably judging my dietary choices. When breakfast came up, I played the classic "Oh, I'm not that hungry" card, which she saw right through. She shoved a plate of food at me anyway, which I gratefully accepted because arguing with her is like arguing with gravity—you're not going to win.

This trip isn't just about visiting family; it's a reconnection with everything simple, chaotic, and heartwarming about small-town life. Sure, there are stairs designed by sadists and train crowds that test the limits of human decency, but there's also a warmth here, a reminder that life isn't just about deadlines and hustle. It's about Coco's relentless enthusiasm, my aunt's overfeeding tendencies, and the way Bokaro feels like a hug you didn't know you needed.

Haggling 101: Bokaro Style

Bokaro's City Center Market is the kind of place that sticks to your memory like *samosa* oil on your fingers—messy, unapologetic, and impossible to wipe away. It's not some fancy, air-conditioned mall with glossy floors and overpriced coffee; no, this place is a circus of life. Stalls groan under the weight of fruits, vegetables, and enough spices to knock out an elephant with a single whiff. The air is a symphony of smells—egg rolls, *bhel puri* (popular Indian street food made from a mixture of puffed rice, tamarind water, and spices), *samosas* frying, *pakoras* (Indian fritters) sizzling, and the occasional hint of "is that...burnt plastic?" wafting in from God-knows-where!

But the real entertainment? The haggling. It's not just commerce; it's theater. Every transaction feels like a Bollywood epic. Vendors say prices that sound like they're auctioning off gold, while buyers react like they've just been told their favorite cricket team lost. There's head-shaking, eye-rolling, and dramatic sighs so synchronized it's almost an art form.

Meanwhile, my aunt? Oh, she's the undisputed queen of this chaos. She strides through the market like she owns the place, her *saree* (dress worn by Indian women which consists of long cloth draped around the body) swishing with the kind of confidence that makes even the mangoes stand a little taller. Vendors call her *"Didi"* (sister) with a mix of respect and mild terror because they know she's about to haggle them into submission. "How much?" She asks with a raised eyebrow that could make the stock market crash, and just like that, the dance begins. She doesn't yell or wave her arms around—she's like a stealth bomber, dropping quiet but deadly lines like, "Are you selling fish or gold?"

And speaking of fish, the fish market is where the real magic happens. The smell hits you first—like the ocean decided to throw a house party and forgot to clean up afterward. It's part saltwater, part fresh catch, and part... let's just call it "character." My aunt glides through puddles of fish guts like she's walking a red carpet, inspecting fish like they've applied for a job in her kitchen. The vendors grumble, but they know better than to mess with her. One poor guy tried to upsell her once; she stared at him until he practically had paid her to take the fish.

Last but not the least, we hit the household goods shop. My aunt was still in full command mode, tossing utensils and spices into her bag like she was stocking up for the apocalypse. Even there, she had that glint in her eye—the look of a woman who had won every round of "Market Olympics" without breaking a sweat.

As the Sun dipped lower, the market began to quiet down. The golden evening light made everything look like an Instagram filter called "Nostalgia." The haggling faded, replaced by the thud of closing shutters and the murmur of tired vendors counting their day's earnings.

It was not glamorous, and it was definitely not quiet, but there was something about it that felt...alive.

Bokaro's market doesn't try to impress you—it just is. A little rough, a little chaotic, but completely authentic. And as we walk out, bags full of everything from mangoes to mops, I can't help but think: this wasn't just a market. It was a comedy show, a time capsule, and a life lesson all rolled into one. Sure, it was imperfect, but that's what made it perfect in its own ridiculous way.

A Flavorful Journey Through Bokaro's Belly

As we made our way back home, the cool air slapped me in the face like it was trying to remind me who's boss. It was not just cold—it was personal too. It was the kind of chill that felt like it's reaching into your soul and rearranging furniture. Bokaro's ever-present hum, which usually sounded like a mix of distant traffic and someone arguing over chai, began to fade. Now it was just us and the gravel crunching beneath our feet, like some overly dramatic scene in an indie movie. The light was fading away, and the air felt heavy, like the Universe was bracing itself for a plot twist.

When we got home, though, all that existential brooding went out the window because there was a plate of hot *samosas* waiting for me! Hot *samosas* had this magical ability to shut down all your deeper thoughts and replace them with, "Oh my god, this is amazing." I bite into one, and it's like a symphony of crispy, spicy goodness explodes in my mouth. The heat of the filling works its way down, warming me up better than any sweater ever could. The spice sneaks up on me—not the kind that leaves you gasping for water but the kind that makes you go, "Yeah, I can handle this," even though your nose is starting to run. Bokaro's *samosas* aren't trying to win any awards. There's no celebrity chef behind them, no secret truffle oil drizzle. Just a humble, crunchy shell with a perfectly spicy filling that feels like it's giving you a hug from the inside. It's like comfort food on steroids. And just when you think you've peaked with samosas, the conversation inevitably turns to *litti chokha.*

Now, *litti chokha* is a whole other ball game. It is a traditional Bihari dish consisting of *"litti"* (wheat flour dough balls stuffed with roasted gram flour and spices) and *"chokha"* (mashed roasted vegetables like eggplant, tomato, and potato). It's not my first choice—I mean, give me fried over roasted any day—but there's something about the whole process that keeps me hooked. Watching *litti* being made is like watching someone perform a ritual passed down from their ancestors. Little dough balls stuffed with *sattu* (flour made by grinding various cereals) are thrown into an open flame like they're tiny sacrifices to the fire gods. The smell of burning wood fills the air, mixing with the spices, and suddenly it feels like you've been transported to a time when life was simpler and nobody knew what kale was. The *litti* itself is kind of a rebel. It doesn't care about looking perfect. The outside gets charred and crispy, and the inside? Soft, nutty, and somehow still manages to taste like a warm hug from the earth. It's messy, unpredictable, and doesn't give a single care about precision. The flames lick around it like they've got their own agenda, and honestly, watching it cook feels like you're witnessing nature and food having a little argument. It reminds me of roasting chicken back in the U.S., but *litti's* got this wild energy to it. Roasting chicken feels civilized—controlled heat, predictable results. *Litti's* like, "Hold my chai, watch this." It's chaotic and smoky, and when you finally take a bite with the tangy *chokha,* it's like the fire and spice got together and decided to throw a party in your mouth. There's no fanfare around it, no Instagram- worthy plating. It's food that doesn't try too hard. And yet, it delivers a lesson without even meaning to: sometimes, the best things in life are a little rough around the edges, a little unpredictable, but completely authentic.

Sharing *litti chokha,* or even just eating a perfectly crisp samosa, feels like you're tapping into something timeless. In a world that's sprinting toward the next big thing, it's moments like these— grounded, real, and delicious—that remind you to slow down. And if slowing down means biting into another *samosa,* well, I'm all in.

A Colorful Mess: The Bokaro Holi Experience

Holi is like the world deciding to hit "shuffle" on its emotions—a chaotic, colorful explosion where nothing makes sense, but somehow everything feels just right. It's not just an Indian festival of colors; it's a beautifully unhinged therapy session for a subcontinent. The air is thick with laughter, the scent of flowers, and—let's be honest—a suspicious hint of *bhaang* (a mild preparation of marijuana made from young leaves and stems of the Indian hemp plant, Cannabis sativa and drunk with milk).

The streets? They're a war zone of music, water balloons, and people whose faces look like a painter's palette gone rogue. There's something magical about how *Holi* levels the playing field; one minute you're dodging water bombs, and the next, your boss is smearing magenta on your cheeks like a giddy teenager. It's a reminder that even the darkest days can be rinsed clean with a bucket of water and an unreasonable amount of neon powder.

At its heart, the act of throwing colors during *Holi* is an art form—a complicated mix of aim, enthusiasm, and unspoken revenge. For me, it always starts the same way: my family gearing up like we're entering a gladiator ring. My dad, the picture of stoicism on every other day, approaches the piles of color like they've personally offended him. His first handful of powder is thrown with the energy of a man who's just been told he has to work on *Holi*, landing on my mom's shoulder with all the precision of a drunk dart player.

There's laughter, sure, but also that unspoken family vibe: Who's going to bring up that argument from last week first? Spoiler alert: It's usually him. My mom, in her pristinely draped sari— because, of course, she didn't get the "Holi is messy" memo—starts off dignified. But the second someone flings pink at her, it's like something snaps. She transforms into a powder-slinging ninja, turning our courtyard into a Jackson Pollock painting. The *sari?* Forget it. It's now a tie-dye masterpiece, and every splash of color is her silent declaration that "I'm done with your nonsense today, kids."

Then there's my sister, who takes *Holi* way too seriously. Armed with a water gun that looks suspiciously military-grade, she charges into battle like it's her personal vendetta. She doesn't just throw color—she hurls it, often with an evil laugh that makes you question her life choices. Her targets? Everyone. Her enthusiasm is contagious, but there's also a faint whiff of, "I've been waiting all year to pelt you with this." Her wild laughter echoes through the house, and while her joy seems infinite, you can't help but think: Is she okay? Or is this some kind of primal scream therapy?

And then there's my aunt—the festival's designated instigator. She doesn't just throw colors; she flings them with the reckless abandon of someone who's already decided she'll deal with the laundry later. Her laughter fills the air like a soundtrack to the madness, but every now and then, she pauses, lost in thought, as if the swirling chaos is reminding her of some bittersweet memory. It's almost poetic— except for the moment she absentmindedly smears blue on her own face, forgetting she's holding a fistful of powder.

As the day unfolds, the chaos reaches peak absurdity. Our once-crisp white outfits now look like they were tie-dyed by a hyperactive toddler. The courtyard is a battlefield of colors, laughter, and occasionally someone yelling, "NOT THE HAIR!" Each burst of powder feels like a tiny rebellion against the mundane, but it's also a weirdly honest expression of everything we're too polite to say out loud. By the end, the vibrant colors don't just coat us—they highlight every laugh, every moment of hesitation, every unspoken thing we carry.

Holi isn't just about color—it's about contradiction. It's messy and freeing, chaotic and introspective, ridiculous and profound. It's a reminder that sometimes, the best way to deal with life's layers is to throw powder at them and hope for the best. And when the madness finally fades, and you're left scrubbing color out of places you didn't know existed, you realize: this is what joy looks like—messy, fleeting, and absolutely worth it.

Bokaro's Quirky Chronicles: A Love-Hate Relationship

Life in Bokaro is like that one relative who hugs you tightly while also whispering, "*Beta* (son), don't trust anyone." It's a place of dazzling duality, where the streets buzz with warmth and laughter but also hide enough suspicion to fuel a decade's worth of crime thrillers.

On one side of the coin, the people of Bokaro share an unspoken bond that can feel like being part of an enormous, dysfunctional family. You'll find everyone knows everyone—down to your childhood nickname, which they will gleefully yell across a crowded market to your eternal embarrassment. Anonymity? What's that? Blink too loud, and half the neighborhood will know about it by evening *chai* (milktea).

Friendships in Bokaro are like those fancy desserts with a hidden center—sweet on the outside but always holding a surprise. People will greet you like you're a long-lost sibling, slap your back hard enough to dislocate a vertebra, and invite you over for dinner with promises of unlimited *gulab jamun* (a popular milk-solid-based sweet, consisting of fried dough balls soaked in rose-scented sugar syrup). But behind the smiles, there's an unspoken audition happening. "Is this person worth trusting? Or should I file this encounter under 'potential gossip content?'" Words whispered in confidence have a funny way of turning into the town's latest headline, complete with dramatic reenactments. It's a place where your deepest secrets might accidentally star in the community's evening entertainment.

Yet, here's the paradox—when life throws you a curveball, these same people who might've discussed your life like it's a TV soap will show up for you like the Avengers assembling. Weddings? They'll dance like it's their cardio routine for the year. Housewarmings? They'll shower your walls with so many blessings you might need a mop. And in grief, their hugs feel like weighted blankets of empathy. Their loyalty during these moments is unmatched—though let's not rule out the possibility of someone subtly critiquing your choice of funeral snacks.

But the other side of Bokaro's coin is a fortress of mistrust, a wall so tall it could give the Great Wall of China an inferiority complex. It's as if everyone's operating on an internal checklist titled "How to Trust Without Really Trusting." This is not paranoia; it's tradition. Parents pass down their prized cookware and this age-old wisdom: "Beta (son), trust no one. Especially that aunty who compliments your garden too much." The mistrust isn't without flair—it's dramatic, relentless, and as deeply ingrained as the taste of mustard oil in Bokaro's cuisine. It's almost poetic: a closeness that binds, yet a guardedness that keeps everyone just a little apart.

The streets of Bokaro resonate with the laughter of shared lives and the whispers of suspicion. Every interaction is a high- stakes game of emotional poker, where people smile warmly but keep their metaphorical cards close to their chests.

In the end, life in Bokaro is an intricate dance of connection and caution. It's where every smile is a mix of sincerity and subtle espionage, every friendship walks the tightrope between trust and a raised eyebrow, and every moment shared feels like both an embrace and a test. But hey, at least the gossip is top-tier entertainment!

If Bokaro were a person...

When I think about Bokaro as a person, I imagine myself standing before a man molded by time and toil. His presence looms like a titan, crafted from the very steel he helps forge. His hands, rough and calloused, tell stories of countless hours spent in the relentless heat of the steel plants. I can almost feel the coarse texture as I imagine shaking his hand, a grip firm and reassuring.

His eyes, a piercing shade of steel blue, hold a depth of experience that makes me pause. They've witnessed the rise and fall of industries, the ebb and flow of prosperity. There's a flicker of something almost ancient in those eyes, as if they've seen and endured more than a lifetime's worth of trials. They pierce through the façade of everyday concerns, reminding me of the enduring human spirit.

His voice, when he speaks, is a deep rumble, resonating like the steady hum of machinery. Each word carries the weight of unspoken wisdom, learned not from books but from the raw, unfiltered experiences of life. It's the kind of voice that commands attention, yet there's a surprising warmth to it, a gentle undercurrent of kindness that invites trust.

I picture his clothing as practical and worn, a heavy jacket that's seen countless winters, and boots that have trudged through the dust and grime of progress. In his jacket pocket, there's a notebook, dog-eared and filled with sketches and notes—blueprints of dreams yet to be realized. It's a small, tangible piece of his relentless drive for innovation, a testament to his enduring hope.

Leaving Bokaro

Leaving Bokaro feels like saying goodbye to a world unto itself. The three-hour drive to the airport in nearby state capital of Ranchi city, allows that to sink in. Seeing all of Jharkhand pass by bestows a sense of sadness in me, as if I'm parting with a living, breathing entity. The landscape, with its dense forests and rolling hills, flashes by, each tree and rock a silent witness to my departure. The earthy scent of the soil, mingled with the faint aroma of roadside *chai*, lingers in the air, a bittersweet reminder of home.

As the car speeds along the winding roads, I catch glimpses of small villages, their thatched roofs peeking out from the greenery. Children play by the roadside, their laughter a fleeting echo in the wind. The vibrant colors of the local markets blur together, life that seems both distant and intimately familiar. The Sun begins to set, casting a golden hue over the landscape. Shadows stretch long and thin, like the memories I'll carry with me.

The rhythmic hum of the car's engine and the gentle sway of the journey create a hypnotic trance, a liminal space where past and present merge. Every mile takes me further away from the heart of Jharkhand. The feeling of leaving is profound, a deep ache that resonates within me. It's more than just a journey; it's a passage, a transition from one world to another, filled with the weight of the uncertainty that lies ahead.

What do I carry from Bokaro?

Bokaro, with its steel-driven energy, is where I learned about my dad's past and the environment that shaped his journey. Though I didn't live there, my visits to Bokaro revealed the essence of the place—its steel industry, its enduring sense of purpose, and the steady hum of progress that defines the city. It's where my dad's roots lie, where his work ethic was cultivated, and where his life took shape amidst the ongoing rhythm of the steel mills. My visits to Bokaro gave me a glimpse into the foundation of my dad's own resilience and determination.

While the city itself is relentless, it also taught me the value of persistence and hard work. But beyond the industry and the bustling pace, my trips to Bokaro also carried moments of calm—sitting with my family in the cool evenings, reflecting on what it meant to build a future. Those visits helped shape my understanding that even in a city of constant movement, there's space for quiet reflection and connection.

Bokaro showed me the value of hard work and persistence and instilled in me a sense of drive.

Though I didn't live in Bokaro, my visits shaped my understanding of who I am and where I come from.

Padri: Rural Rhythms

Padri is a quaint village in the Indian state of Bihar, characterized by its serene landscapes and a tight-knit community bound by age-old traditions.

Nestled amidst lush greenery, it captures the simplicity and rustic charm of rural India. It serves as a vivid reflection of rural life, where fields stretch endlessly, and age-old customs coexist with whispers of modernity trying to find a foothold. While its scenic beauty and the heartfelt, trusting aspirations of its people paint a picture of openness and hope, a quiet caution lingers beneath the surface—gently shaping their interactions and revealing the intricate complexities of village life.

Arriving: Can a place remember you?

The car's rumble grew softer as we approached Padri, its wheels bouncing steadily over uneven roads. That moment felt like homecoming, the car felt like a thread connecting us to something bigger than the present—a return to roots, a reconnection to what once was. My mother adjusted her *saari,* something she wears religiously only when she visits Padri, as a sign of respect to the culture and its people. In the back seat, her gaze is calm but intent as she watches the familiar fields roll past. Even without speaking, it was clear Padri held a quiet weight over her, as if the village carried pieces of her journey that words could never fully capture. Or maybe it was just the fact that she'd forgotten her phone charger and was getting slightly irritated by thinking about it.

My father sat in the front; his gaze fixed on the narrow road ahead. There was something reflective about his stillness. Padri wasn't just a place for him; it was his roots-his real home in this world, or maybe just the place where he learned how to dodge cows on the road.

The road narrowed further, the green crops flanking either side swaying gently in the breeze. Villagers walked alongside the road, stopping now and then to talk or adjust the loads balanced on their heads. My elder sister leaned forward in her seat, her sharp eyes scanning for ways to cut through the slow-moving carts and herding cows. She was the practical one, always focused on the next step, even here where time seemed to move at its own pace. Meanwhile, my baby brother, nestled against my mother, was wide-eyed with wonder. Every sight, every sound—be it the clatter of pots or the rhythmic chanting of women walking home—seemed to hold his attention. He didn't yet understand that this place was part of his heritage, but his tiny hands reaching for the window as if to grab hold of the moment said more than words ever could. Or maybe he just really liked the sound of cows mooing.

When we finally got out of the car, the first thing I felt was the air—thicker here, filled with smells of wet earth and wood smoke. It was also slightly overpowered by the unmistakable scent of my father's aftershave, which still lingered from when we got in the car. The houses, their walls worn with age, seemed to lean into the dusty roads, proud of their resilience. It wasn't just a village; it was history standing still, waiting to be remembered. Padri wasn't perfect, but it was home in a way that defied explanation. Each visit felt like rediscovering something we didn't know we had lost.

The First Bite of Khichdi—A Taste of Home

We sat around the table, the wooden surface rough under our hands. The oil lamp flickered in the corner, casting shadows on the walls.

Food in Padri wasn't just something to fill your stomach—it was part of the adventure of the day. The *khichdi* was simple: rice, lentils, cumin, and ghee. The flavors weren't complicated, but they were enough. The cumin, fried in ghee, brought warmth to the dish, and the mango pickle on the side was the cherry on top, bringing the dish together—kind of like that one aunt who's always shouting, "Have another helping!" at family gatherings. The curd provided a cooling balance to the spice, making each bite satisfying. It was a meal we had many times, yet every time felt like the first.

My baby brother, too young to understand much, giggled as he reached for the food with messy hands. Watching him reminded me that this meal was as much about tradition as it was about the people who shared it. It wasn't just food—it was a way to be connected to the place and to each other. His laugh, simple and pure, was like a small reminder that life in Padri was built on moments like these.

My sister ate quietly, taking small bites and seeming to savor every taste, her focus on the food. She wasn't one to rush, and even in a simple meal like this, she seemed to appreciate it in her own way. Mostly by eyeing my plate to see if I was going to eat that last piece of *khichdi*.

The rest of us ate at our usual pace—no rush, just the comfort of a meal we knew well. There was a calm in the way we ate, a sense that food here was about more than just filling up. It was about being in this place, surrounded by the people you know best.

After we finished eating, the room fell into a brief silence. The plates were empty, but the feeling of the meal lingered. We didn't need to speak—it was enough to sit there, knowing that we had shared something that was part of the fabric of Padri. It was about the simplicity, the routine, and the comfort of eating something familiar in a place that felt like it held the weight of every meal shared here before. It wasn't just about nourishment; it was about belonging—and about hoping there would be some leftover *khichdi* for one more round.

Shopping: The Green Bangles of Padri Market

Padri's market wasn't just a world—it was an entire universe unto itself. The market went on and on as though it were infinite. The moment we entered, we were enveloped in a mix of sounds—vendors shouting prices, customers haggling, children laughing. It was loud, but not chaotic; there was a tune to the place, a shared understanding of how it all worked, kind of like a Bollywood (Indian popular film industry, based in Mumbai (Bombay)) movie, but with fewer dance numbers.

My aunt led the way, balancing my baby brother on her hip while navigating the crowded aisles. Her bargaining was sharp and efficient, she had a way of cutting prices without cutting respect. At one stall, she tested tomatoes for ripeness, at another, she negotiated over a pile of coconuts. Every purchase seemed deliberate, a result of eons of experience.

My father didn't say much, but he didn't need to. A simple nod from him at a vendor's stall seemed to carry more weight than any number of words. It was the power of' Dad Nod', a move perfected over years of marriage.

My sister, meanwhile, lingered at the fabric stalls, her fingers tracing the soft cottons and shimmering silks. She wasn't buying; she was imagining—every fabric a possible steppingstone for a future endeavor. Or a future outfit for the next wedding we attend.

Then we found the jewelry stall. My baby brother reached for a set of bright green bangles hanging from a hook, his tiny fingers curling around them. My mother jingled them for him, and his delighted laughter made heads turn. For a moment, the stall, the noise, and the crowd faded, leaving just the three of us sharing a small, joyful moment.

The market wasn't a page in a book; it required a whole chapter. It was where the village's chronicles unfolded—every transaction, every interaction, another thread in the fabric of Padri's life. Even as we left, I could still hear the hum of it, like an echo that follows you wherever you go. Or at least until we got to the car and the noise of my baby brother's cries drowned everything out.

Janmashtami: A Celebration of Village Unity

Janmashtami is annual Hindu festival in India which celebrates the birth of Lord Krishna. The festival's buildup started hours before it began. The Krishna temple of the village, usually quiet and simple, had been transformed. Marigold garlands were draped over the stone pillars, and strings of fairy lights sparkled in the dusky evening. The air was thick with the scent of incense and the earthy smell of the village—a mix that seemed to hang heavy with anticipation, or maybe it was just the amount of sweat in the air from running around. By late evening, the village had come alive. Women emerged from their homes, draped in bright saris of every color—emerald greens, saffron, and vibrant reds. Children, their faces smeared with turmeric and their feet bare, ran across the village square, their laughter echoing in the night.

The streets, usually calm, were now a blur of movement, the pace quickened by the shared excitement. The usual stillness of Padri had given way to an undercurrent of energy. The *Dahi Handi* event, the centerpiece of the celebration, was drawing everyone's attention. It was a reenactment of Krishna's playful attempts to steal curd and butter, which was kept at an unreachable height by his foster mother Yashoda.

A pot of curd and butter was suspended high above the village square, and young men began to form human pyramids to reach it. They climbed one by one, their hands gripping shoulders, balancing with precision, while the crowd below cheered them on.

My father stood with us, but his eyes weren't on the pot. He was watching the young men, his expression steady but thoughtful, perhaps remembering his own youth, maybe seeing a bit of himself in their effort. Or just thinking about how he would've fallen off that pyramid in 2 seconds flat.

The cheers grew louder as the human pyramid reached the pot's height, broke it open, spilling curd and butter over themselves and onto the ground. The crowd erupted to applause. The moment felt like a collective release, a shared joy that went beyond the festival itself. Everyone in the crowd, from the youngest child to the oldest villager, felt the victory.

The essence of the event was more than reaching the pot, it was about what that effort symbolized: the strength of the community, the unity they found in the challenge.

As the evening progressed, the *bhajans* (religious devotional hymns) began. The village priest led the *bhajan* with his voice rising above the crowd, steady and commanding. The rhythm of the chants felt familiar, almost like the pulse of Padri itself. People closed their eyes, swayed gently, and raised their hands in devotion. Even my baby brother, still too young to understand the significance, clapped his hands to the beat, his giggles joining the chorus of the village's celebration.

Janmashtami wasn't just a religious festival. It was a reminder of the shared life of Padri—its joys, its struggles, its collective spirit. It was about how everyone, in their own way, became part of something larger than themselves. Or about how everyone really looked at the pot of curd as the promise of success and prosperity that the entire village collectively pursued to get a better life for all its people.

People: A Village of Extended Family

The people of Padri lived as if they were all part of one giant, slightly dysfunctional, extended family. There was always time for one another, even if you didn't ask for it. Conversations didn't happen with urgency; they were more like long, winding roads that had no destination—and no one cared. Time in Padri didn't just move slowly, it threw on a hammock, grabbed a *chai* (tea), and took a nap in the afternoon Sun. Even if you weren't technically family, it felt like you were. If you didn't know someone, don't worry, you would, by the end of the day. The neighbors didn't just wave as they passed; they'd plant themselves in front of you, make small talk about your grandmother's health, the color on your walls, and offer you *chai* like you had nothing better to do. And honestly, you didn't. You'd often walk by someone's house and find the door wide open, as if to say, "Come in, help yourself to whatever's in the fridge. If it's the neighbor's fridge, even better!" It wasn't a matter of privacy; it was a matter of how much of your life you could squeeze into five minutes.

In Padri, the idea of community wasn't something you casually participated in; it was something you were born into—whether you liked it or not. If someone needed help, whether it was lifting heavy things, offering advice on how to remove a stubborn stain, or just hearing about how their cow had mysteriously disappeared, help was handed out like candy. No formalities needed.

People shared meals like they were playing a game of "take what you need, but leave the last piece for the person who probably forgot to come for dinner." Celebrations didn't just belong to the person having the event; if there was a wedding, a birthday, or even a random Tuesday, the whole village was invited, whether they were prepared or not. It wasn't just kindness; it was more like a well-practiced habit. A village that thrived on the idea that if one person was thriving, everyone was legally obligated to join in, even if it was just to eat cake.

The older folks—those who had seen Padri's glorious days—held on to these traditions like they were the last piece of mango pickle in the jar, even if the younger generation had their eyes glued to their phones and weren't as invested in the "all-in-this-together" mentality. But the belief stuck around. No one ever really left. And that was the beauty of it. Padri wasn't just a place to live; it was a 24/7 reality show where you were always the star—and the audience.

If Padri were a person...

If Padri were a person, it would be an old yet ageless man—someone who seemed ancient, yet ageless, carrying with him the stories of time immemorial. His face would be gracefully old with still a lot of glow, etched deeply with lines that marked the passing of decades, of struggles and celebrations, of monsoons and droughts. His skin would be like parchment, dry and crinkled, but still resilient, still strong, still holding onto the life within him. His eyes—dark and deep—would gaze out from under heavy lids, watching the world with a mixture of knowing and acceptance. There would be no rush in his movements, no need to keep up with the fast pace of the modern world. He had seen it all before, in some form or another, and he knew that everything eventually circled back, that time was less a straight line and more an ever-turning wheel.

He would sit under the banyan tree at the edge of the village, the same tree that had seen generations come and go. His presence there would feel timeless, like he had always been and would always be, an integral part of the village, as much a fixture as the land itself.

His clothes, worn but clean, would speak of a life lived simply but purposefully. He wouldn't care much for appearances—it didn't matter, after all, he had spent his entire life working the land, feeling the soil between his fingers, sowing seeds and reaping harvests. His hands, rough and calloused from years of labor, would move slowly, but with the graceful ease of someone who knew the value of patience, of waiting for things to grow in their own time.

He wouldn't speak much—there would be no need to. His silence would say more than words could. But when he did speak, his voice would be soft, almost gravelly, like the sound of wind moving through the fields. His stories wouldn't be grand or embellished; they would be simple, understated, but filled with the weight of experience. He would tell you about the drought of '76, or the best harvest the village ever had, or the time when the river overflowed and changed the course of the land. His tales wouldn't be just about history; they would be lessons, passed down through the generations, reminding that the past was never truly gone. It lived on in the land, in the people, in the very air of the village. If you sat with him long enough, you would feel it too—that connection to something greater, something older than yourself.

In his presence, you would become acutely aware of the cycles of life, of how everything was connected, how the past bled into the present, and how the future would carry pieces of both. Padri, in his form, would be a constant—a quiet, enduring strength that stood firm as the world changed around him. In his company, you would feel small but not insignificant, as though you were part of a larger story, one that had been written long before you and would continue long after.

This old man wouldn't try to impress you. He wouldn't dazzle you with tales of heroism or adventure. But in his quiet way, he would ground you, remind you of where you came from, of the soil that nourished your roots. He would teach you, without saying a word, that there is beauty in endurance, in persistence, in simply being. In his gaze, you would find a reflection of Padri itself—a village that had stood the test of time, always changing yet always the same, a place that existed not just on a map, but within the hearts of those who had ever called it home.

Leaving Padri, But Never Really Leaving

Leaving Padri was never simple. It wasn't a vacation; it was slow and reluctant farewell.

Mom folded her *saris* carefully, taking extra time to smooth each crease, as though the act of folding could keep Padri with her just a little longer. Dad stood near the doorway, his eyes scanning the courtyard, lingering on the mango tree that had been there for as long as he could remember. For him, it was more than just a tree; it was a marker of time. Or maybe it was just the best spot for shade in the summer.

My sister didn't say much. She stood by the door, arms crossed, her gaze lingering on the small details—the scratches on the walls (caused by yours truly), the familiar worn paths in the courtyard. She wasn't one to show emotion, but even she seemed caught in the moment, unwilling to leave completely.

And then there was my baby brother, oblivious to everything, his giggles ringing out as he reached for anything and everything in sight. He would never understand the significance of this moment, but in his innocence, there was a reminder that the world kept turning, regardless of our attachments.

As the car drove away, the village shrank in the rearview mirror, the familiar roads fading into the distance. But somehow, Padri felt closer than ever, like a memory you can't forget, no matter how far you go.

What do I carry from Padri?

Padri is a village where time and patience shape everything. It's a place where people are connected like an extended family, and everyone has time for each other. But trust isn't given freely— because of past betrayals and old wounds. Hence it needs to be earned, slowly. Relationships here aren't rushed; they're built over time through small, consistent actions.

This environment taught me that trust is something that grows gradually and that true connection takes effort and patience. Living in Padri shaped how I view relationships, teaching me the value of time and care in building trust, and how even in a close community, people can remain guarded. It showed me that real understanding and trust aren't automatic—they take time, and that's how bonds are formed and maintained. That's what it taught me and shaped the person I have become.

Part II

Ellicott City: A Haven of Stillness

Ellicott City is located in Howard County, in the state of Maryland, USA. It sits along the Patapsco River, blending rural charm with suburban convenience. For me, it's more than just a town—it's my second home. After moving from India in 2018, my family and I settled here, finding a sense of belonging and a fresh start. The peaceful streets and tight-knit community were contrasting to my dynamic life back in Delhi, India. Ellicott City holds a unique place in my journey, representing a quiet space for introspection. It's a reminder that home can be wherever you find a balance between roots and new horizons.

Arriving in the Suburban Jungle

So, in 2018, we pulled into Ellicott City like a family of curious aliens who had just crash-landed in a pristine, almost unnervingly perfect suburban neighborhood. The journey was a blur, mostly because the only thing running through my head was: Where the heck are we, and why do I feel like we're in some bizarre, low-budget reality show where everything is supposed to look normal, but something's definitely off?

My dad, trying to maintain the appearance of a competent driver, was gripping the wheel like it was the last lifeline to some kind of suburban survival, while my mom, ever the optimist, peered out the window like she was deciphering an ancient code hidden in the perfectly trimmed hedges. Yes, this is home now, she probably thought, as if the neatly mowed lawns could somehow distract her from the deep existential crisis we were all quietly having.

I was in the backseat, my mind doing mental gymnastics as I tried to process what I was seeing: cookie-cutter houses with perfectly symmetrical windows and doors, lawns that looked like they were being cut by microscopic robots, and the faintest sound of windchimes tinkling somewhere in the distance. I half expected to hear an eerie voice from a PA system saying, "Welcome to Ellicott City, where everything is perfect and your soul is optional." My sister, ever the phone addict, was probably sending Snapchat stories of "how weird" everything was, using captions like "I feel like I'm living in a 2000s sitcom."

When we finally stopped in front of our new apartment, I had to remind myself to breathe, because this was it. The place where we would live, breathe, eat, and probably never question the fact that it looked like a set design for "How to be a Middle-Class Suburbanite: The Movie." The apartment was... sterile, not in a chic, minimalist way, but more as if someone had deliberately scrubbed all the soul out of it. The walls were beige, the air was beige, even the light coming through the windows felt beige. I honestly thought the place might have been haunted by the ghosts of forgotten décor choices.

My mom, in her infinite wisdom, threw a family photo on the windowsill, probably to "add some personality." But let's be real. The beige walls were like the Universe's way of saying, "Don't bother trying to decorate; you'll only be disappointed."

My dad started to check every window, lock, and possible escape route in a very suspicious manner, almost like he expected a break-in from a rogue squad of suburban burglars who specialized in "taking people's stuff while they're innocently trimming their hedges." I swear, he was one second away from giving a detailed analysis of how the security system could be improved.

Meanwhile, my sister was doing what she did best—avoidance. She had already locked herself in her room, most likely plotting her next existential crisis over whether to get a second-hand desk or a brand-new one. And me? I stood there, taking it all in. The smell of fresh wood and plastic was overwhelming, and I could already feel the existential dread building up like a storm cloud in my chest. If I didn't have a sense of humor, I would have broken down right then and there, but instead, I took a mental note to start wearing more beige clothing to fit in.

From Daal to Kale: A Culinary Tragedy

By the time we made it to dinner that night, I had already given up on the idea of comfort food. My mom, in her infinite wisdom, cooked *daal* and rice. She tried to make it taste like the real thing—like the *daal* we would have eaten back home in India with such gusto that even the hottest, spiciest dish couldn't compete. But there was one little problem. It didn't taste like home. Not at all. It tasted like an amateur's attempt at Indian food. You know what I'm talking about? The kind of *daal* that's made with the wrong kind of lentils or the spices that only make a cameo appearance after you've been looking for them for five minutes. The cumin was barely there. The turmeric didn't even try to show up on stage. The garlic, instead of wafting through the air like a glorious greeting, sort of sulked in the background like it had been grounded for being too bold.

I sat at the table, staring at the rice, which, in an unfortunate twist of fate, had somehow become the star of the show. It was the type of rice that wasn't fluffy, wasn't sticky, and definitely wasn't going to win any awards for its texture. It was, in fact, the kind of rice you'd get if you forgot to turn the stove on for a few minutes—undercooked, underwhelming, and, for some reason, far too committed to being dry.

I could see the pain in my dad's eyes as he chewed through his *daal,* because even he, who normally had the tolerance of a saint, could sense something was wrong. This wasn't the hearty, comforting *daal* of our homeland. This was a sad, mild-mannered immitation that didn't deserve the title of *daal*. It was like the evil twin that had been banished from the family reunion.

Meanwhile, my sister was texting about how the whole dinner experience was, probably to her friends back home, detailing how the *daal* was "not spicy enough" and how "weird" the whole thing felt. She was probably also sharing a picture of the *daal* with the caption, "Can we just skip to the pizza part?"

Oh, pizza! I could already feel it calling out to me. I'll admit, I became hopeful. We ordered pizza because that's what you do when you don't know what else to do, right? You embrace the "American Culture". The pizza arrived, and when I opened the box, I was confronted with the very essence of disappointment. It was a sad, limp dough circle, topped with cheese that looked like it had been carefully placed in the "dare to eat" section. The crust was crunchy in the wrong way—more like cardboard pretending to be bread. The sauce tasted like ketchup was having an identity crisis. The cheese was… well, let's just say it was the type of cheese that made you wonder if anyone had even bothered to make it taste good. As I chewed through the crust, I wondered how something so universally adored could taste like it had been created in an alternate universe where food had no flavor. The pizza felt like the culinary equivalent of a bore—the kind of person who talks about their day at work for hours and somehow makes even the most thrilling parts sound boring. But I had to keep chewing, because the alternative was facing the harsh reality that we weren't in India anymore, and pizza was as close as I was going to get to comfort food.

The food in Ellicott City wasn't terrible, just that it lacked that spirit—the "liveliness" of Indian food.

The Great Grocery Store Escapade

Ellicott City was supposed to be our second chance. A quiet, suburban town, or as I like to call it, "America's Waiting Room." It was pristine—so pristine, it felt like I was living in an Ikea showroom. We were a family of four—Mom, Dad, my elder sister, and me. My baby brother didn't even exist in the cosmic realm of possibility yet; he wouldn't come along until 2021. We were a team, navigating this new land, trying to carve out some semblance of "normal" in a place that was nearly too perfect to be real.

The weekends started the same way every time: with a grocery store trip, Mom's way of "anchoring us to some routine" amidst this strange new land. The grocery store in Ellicott City was nothing like the chaotic, glorious mess of open markets back home in India. There would be no vendors shouting *"Aata, Daal, Haldi!"* (Flour, Pulses, Turmeric!) No bargaining, no haggling, and certainly no earthy smell of coriander wafting through the air. Instead, we would be greeted by aisles of sterile, shiny, pre-packaged perfection. It would be less of a store and more of an episode of "Who Needs So Many Brands of Almond Milk?"

Honestly, the place would be like an Ikea for food—where everything would be arranged with such mathematical precision, that there would be no more soul left to it! It would be filled with aisles upon aisles of, "This is what you should be eating"— quinoa, kale, organic bread that had probably never even touched a grain of wheat, packaged sauces promising "authentic flavor" but not really delivering anything more than a sad apology in a jar. It would feel like food on display at a museum rather than something I was supposed to eat. Each product seemed to scream, "I am perfect, but I'm not sure I'm edible."

Mom, with the intensity of a general leading an army, would push the cart down the aisles with her battle-ready list. She would occasionally stop to consult the "organic" section, where she would find nothing but overpriced herbs and spices that were somehow both too fancy and too bland.

Eventually, we would stumble upon a section that was vaguely familiar—the “Indian Food” aisle! It would feel like a reunion with a distant cousin you only saw at weddings. The bags of *basmati* (a kind of long-grained aromatic rice grown in India) would look comforting, though a bit overpriced.

Then would come the spices section... well, they didn’t really smell like home either; they just kind of sat there, like they were waiting for the magic to happen, but no magician had come around. My mom would buy some *garam masala* (an Indian hot spice mixture), even though she knew it was going to disappoint.

Lentils, rice, vegetables—things that should’ve been as simple as breathing, but here they seemed so complicated. Back home, vegetables were vibrant, fresh, and felt alive in your hand, like they had stories to tell. Here? They would be as perfect as a group photo in a family calendar— no bumps, no bruises, just a uniform shade of green. It would feel like they had been airbrushed.

My sister and I would exchange looks that said, “This is wrong, right? This is so wrong!” Dad, as usual, would remain in his silent Zen mode, nodding or shrugging in approval as Mom agonized over the rice aisle, like it was the final round of a game show. “*Basmati*, Jasmine, Uncle Ben’s... Ahh, none of these are quite right,” she’d say, shaking her head with the determination of someone trying to solve world peace.

Eventually we would make it home with a bag of ‘Indian-American food’, which essentially meant a lot of bland things that would make your taste buds file a formal complaint.

Shopping Malls – Temples of Consumerism

If the grocery store was sterile, the mall would be its hyperactive cousin on a double shot of espresso. Malls would be like temples of consumerism, where I was supposed to worship brands I didn't care about. Marble floors that glistened unnaturally, lights that could double as interrogation lamps, and air thick with the smell of cinnamon pretzels. The stores would stretch out in front of us, offering things we didn't need but were somehow compelled to look at—much like a magic trick that made you say, "Why am I watching this?"

My sister would be the mall's biggest fan. For her, it was a way of pretending—pretending we were part of this world, or at least pretending to understand its unwritten rules. She would drag us into high-end brand stores, flipping through racks of clothes that all seemed to look exactly the same—denim, flannel, and the occasional sparkly top she thought would help her blend in like an American girl on a Netflix show. Mom would stand by, quietly holding the bags. She was a silent martyr to the "let's blend in" cause, eyes betraying the weariness she tried to hide. She knew this wasn't us. But we would play along, because what else could we do?

When everything would be done, we would end up in the food court, the gravitational center of all mall traffic. The scent of fried food and sugar hung thick, as if the mall was saying, "You can't escape indulgence, so let's make it easy." My sister would race toward the pizza counter because, clearly, pizza was the holy grail of American food. I would follow, not because I was hungry but because I had no choice—this was the path of least resistance. We would sit with trays of greasy pizza. Dad would always say, "It's the least offensive option," but I swear, that orange chicken tasted more like a candied nightmare than actual food.

We would eat in relative silence, surrounded by the hum of people who clearly knew how to navigate this world. Families, couples, teenagers—they all seemed like they were living in a movie, and we were extras. The whole thing felt like a montage, but we were stuck at the part where the character is still figuring out what they're supposed to do with their life.

Suburban Festival Syndrome

Ellicott City didn't know what to do with Indian festivals of *Diwali* and *Holi*. It was like bringing a dragon into a petting zoo—it just didn't fit. The town was orderly, structured, and about as lively as a bag of bricks. But here we were, trying to force vibrant, chaotic festivals into a place that barely tolerated the idea of people making noise after 9 PM. Hence these festivals, always felt out of place. Like wearing flip-flops to a black-tie event.

Diwali was the first slap-in-the-face reminder of that difference. Back in India, the anticipation for *Diwali* would build up for weeks—markets alive with chatter, lights everywhere, and streets filled with the sweet smell of treats. In Ellicott City? Nothing. Just a bunch of minivans parked in their tidy driveways, oblivious to the fact that we were supposed to be celebrating. But no matter how it was on the outside, atleast inside our home, we would try to make it feel like India. Mom would light the *diyas* - small cup-shaped oil lamps made of baked clay, that were supposed to bring graceful warmth to the house, but instead, they just flickered weakly against the sterile white walls. It felt lifeless. The quiet outside would be so profound, it would almost feel like the town was holding its breath, unsure of how to react to our noise. But anyways, we would dress up, perform the *puja* (Hindu ceremonial worship involving rituals, chanting and praying), and Mom would prepare all the classic *Diwali* foods— *samosas, laddoos and kheer*. However, the excitement which we would feel back in India, was missing. In India, our house would've been filled with people - friends, relatives, neighbors, anyone and everyone who wanted to come, eat and laugh. But here sadly, it would just be us. Even though our plates would be full of *Diwali* snacks, it would feel tasteless without the warmth of community.

And then there was *Holi* –the festival of colors—pure chaos in India. But in Ellicott City? It would be a ghost town; streets empty, the sky too clear, and everyone just pretending it wasn't happening. But we would try, of course. In the empty backyard of our apartment, my sister and I would smear powdered colors on each other, looking like a tie-dye disaster. Mom would watch us with a smile that looked a bit forced, as if she knew we were trying to re-kindle a festival that didn't fit here. Afterwards, we'd sit down for *Holi* food—*gujiyas* (sweet fried dumplings), *dahi bhallas* (yogurt lentil fritters), things that should've been shared with friends and neighbors. But in Ellicott City? No one would come by. The doorbell would never ring! The laughter wouldn't echo through the streets. It would be just us, sitting at the table with food that tasted like it should have been accompanied by joy, but instead was swallowed down in silence.

And the next day? Guess what! We would be back at the grocery store! Back to the American routine. Back to the same sterile aisles, where every item would sit lifeless.

The bland Muzak would play softly in the background, reminding us that the world moved forward, and we were insignificant.

In the end, no matter how many *diyas* we would light for *Diwali*, or how many colors we would throw in the air for *Holi*, Ellicott City remained a stranger to our vibrant lively festivals. It was a town that gave us safety, but not the joy of celebration. And maybe that's what made it difficult —knowing that while we could find a place to live, we were finding it difficult to truly make it home. We were a family trying to blend in, but it felt like we were still performing in a play with an audience that had already left.

People: The Suburban Enigma

People in Ellicott City have this magical ability to fade into the background. It's not that they're rude or anything, but there's this invisible line that no one dares to cross, like a barrier of politeness you can't touch without being socially exiled. Life here is structured too much—each person neatly slotted into their own routine, compartmentalized, with zero chance of anything chaotic slipping in.

Picture a friendly smile, a nod of acknowledgment, maybe a quick wave from behind perfectly pruned hedges—because in Ellicott City, that's the maximum human connection one can expect. You could live next door to someone for years and not know a single thing about them. It's like living next door to an illusion—a perfectly maintained façade. Take our next-door neighbor Mrs. Delaney (name changed), for example. Her yard was so immaculate it looked like it had been planted by the gods of suburban gardening themselves. Rows of flowers so perfect they probably came with an instruction manual. And yet, behind her polished exterior, Mrs. Delaney was like a ghost. A friendly ghost, sure—but a ghost nonetheless. She'd wave to us with that smile that didn't quite make it past her teeth. There was something off about her, but in the world of Ellicott City, no one even bothered to ask.

Then came the winter of mystery. Snow covered everything like a big, cold blanket, and we noticed something strange: Mrs. Delaney's house was dark and quiet. The lights were out, the chimney was silent. Her yard still stood in military precision. For days. Mom, of course, took it upon herself to be the ray of light that could melt even the iciest of suburban hearts. She sent me to knock on Mrs. Delaney's door, plate of *Holi* sweets in hand. Yes, you read that right—*Holi* sweets in the middle of winter. Only in Ellicott City could you find such cultural confusion!

I knocked. Nothing. Knocked again. The wind howled in response. And then the door creaked open just a crack. Inside, there she was—pale, drawn, staring at me like I'd just woken her from some 20-year coma. She didn't even blink at the sweets. She just looked at me like I was the last person on Earth she expected to see. I didn't know if I should run or call a priest. So, I awkwardly held up the sweets and said, "Mom made these for *Holi,* thought you might want some."

She didn't reach for the plate. Not a single movement. She didn't even look at it. Instead, her gaze flickered over my face, and for a split second, I swear I saw fear—or maybe it was just an aggressive form of suburban guilt. Hard to say. After what felt like an eternity of standing in the cold, she nodded once, then slowly closed the door.

No words. No explanation. Just the door shutting on my face as if I'd somehow broken an unspoken Ellicott City law.

I left, not sure if I'd seen a ghost or just the embodiment of suburbia's soul-crushing monotony. The plate of sweets probably went untouched. We would never know. Because in Ellicott City, to breach this carefully maintained façade was like committing a crime! And I didn't want to be on the other side of this unspoken law, by pointing out that 'something was not right in this town!'

Months later, we came to know that Mrs. Delaney was gone. They said she passed away quietly. I bet her perfectly trimmed garden didn't even flinch. The house was sold. New family, same meticulously planned yard. Life went on. As always. The neighbors drifted in and out of each other's lives, leaving barely a footprint behind. And here's the kicker: no one even talked about it. Because that's the Ellicott City way—polite, distant, and absolutely terrifying if you try to look past the surface.

If Ellicott City were a person...

If Ellicott City were a person, she would be that quiet, composed figure you'd pass on the street without a second glance, her clothes pressed and clean, her smile practiced. She wouldn't say much, but when she did, her words would be measured, never too loud, never too bold. Everything about her would feel deliberate, like she's spent years perfecting the art of blending in, of existing in the background, unnoticed but undeniably present. Her hair would fall in neat, predictable waves, not a strand out of place.

You'd find her at the local coffee shop, sipping something safe—maybe a latte with just the right amount of foam, never anything too daring. She'd have her life sorted, or at least, that's what she'd want you to believe.

She'd own a house with a perfectly manicured lawn, her garden a curated collection of plants that never grow too wild. Everything in her world would be carefully organized, from her spice rack to the photos on her walls, each one framed and positioned with care.

But underneath that veneer of calm, there would be a restlessness. Something unspoken. Ellicott City would have secrets, the kind she'd never share, not even with her closest friends. You'd sense it in the way her eyes sometimes drift off, as if she's thinking of a world beyond the tidy streets she calls home. She'd have seen things, known things, but she wouldn't talk about them. Not openly. Instead, she'd tuck them away, hidden behind layers of suburban politeness, always keeping that part of herself just out of reach.

She'd be dependable, reliable and predictable in the way that made you feel safe. You'd know exactly what to expect from her—she'd never surprise you, never shock you with an outburst or a sudden change of heart. And maybe that's what would make her both comforting and a little sad. Because while she'd be everything you'd want in a friend—steady, predictable, kind—she'd also be someone who never truly let you in.

There'd be moments though, when you'd catch glimpses of something else. A flash of rebellion in her eyes, a quiet longing for something more. Maybe it would come out late at night, after a glass of wine, when her guard would be down. She'd talk about places she's never been, cities she's only dreamed of visiting. She'd confess to wanting more than the life she had built, more than the routine she had so carefully curated. But by morning, she'd be back to her old self, folding the laundry and making grocery lists, pretending that the night before never happened.

Ellicott City, if she were a person, would be someone you could count on. She'd show up when you needed her, always ready with a smile and a helping hand. But deep down, you'd know she's living a life that isn't quite hers. A life that fits the expectations of the world around her, but never really reflects who she is underneath it all. And you'd wonder, sometimes, what she'd be like if she ever let that part of herself out. If she ever stopped pretending.

Leaving Ellicott City - From Silent Suburbia to Complete Chaos

We left Ellicott City and returned to India in 2022. It felt like stepping off a movie set and entering back into the real world. Ellicott City, with its suburban perfection, was like a script everyone followed to the letter. The houses were all "neatly" cast, and the streets felt like a place where even the squirrels adhered to a daily timetable.

But the second you step off that plane in India, the script gets thrown out the window, the actors forget their lines, and chaos takes center stage. At the airport in Maryland, it's all very proper—people stand in line, give you space, and exchange those lovely little "excuse me"s. But the moment you step into an Indian airport, all that goes out the window. The air feels like it's charged with a kind of "get out of my way" energy, and you can already sense that the calm bubble you've been living in is about to pop. Even the flight attendants know it. Before taking off from Ellicott City, they're giving you polite smiles. But later they've got their serious faces on, in preparation for what's coming when the plane's wheels hit the Indian tarmac... and before you know it, BOOM, you land in Delhi!

The air is thick with humidity, the smell of diesel fumes and street food hits you like a brick wall, and it's so strong it feels like the city itself is yelling in your face. Forget about the quietness of Ellicott City. Here, the noise is everywhere: cars honking, vendors yelling and the occasional cow walking by like it owns the place. Your senses are on high alert, and you wonder if you've accidentally landed in a live-action version of Mario Kart.

But the real fun begins on my way to *Nani's* (maternal grandmother's) house in Darbhanga, in the Indian state of Bihar. In Ellicott City, the roads are as calm as a yoga class in a library. Here? It's a vehicular free-for-all. Cars, rickshaws, motorcycles, and random cows all playing a twisted version of musical chairs as they race down the streets. And somehow, it works. Not well, mind you, but it works. When we finally get to her house, it's like stepping into the past. The pond out front is still there, calm and serene, while the house feels like it's refusing to acknowledge any form of modernization. The smells, the sounds—everything is overwhelming, from the sizzling oil in the kitchen to the chaotic chatter of the extended family all trying to talk over each other. It's like walking into a living, breathing version of family drama—and I'm the star of the show whether I like it or not.

Back in Ellicott City, grocery shopping felt like a chore. The store shelves were organized like a military operation, with each product in perfect, symmetrical rows. In India, though, the market is alive—vendors yelling at each other, shouting out prices, and you can practically taste the spice in the air. It's messy, but it feels like you're part of something real, not just a sanitized version of reality.

And the food? Oh, the food. Back in Ellicott City, we ate like robots—predictable, flavorless, safe. But in India, each meal feels like an explosion of flavor in your mouth. Every bite of *roti, daal, sabzi* (flatbreads, cooked lentils, cooked vegetables)—is a reminder that life doesn't have to be bland and predictable but can be chaotic, loud, strong and alive!

And let's talk about festivals. In Ellicott City, *Diwali* was a quiet, private affair—sparklers in the backyard, a few fireworks, and a lot of nervous glances to make sure we didn't set off any fire alarms. But in India? It's a full-on war zone of celebration. Crackers bursting off in every corner, decorative lights strung up on every tree, and smoke so thick you could cut it with a knife. It's beautiful. It's loud. It's real.

And the people? In Ellicott City, they give you a wave, a smile, and keep walking. There's a polite distance, a well-guarded wall between you and everyone else. Whereas in India, people don't wave. They grab you, pull you into their lives, and ask how your entire extended family is doing, even if they've never met them. It's overwhelming. But you know what? It's comforting in its own weird way.

Ellicott City? It's safe. It's predictable. But India? India is the real deal. It's messy, chaotic, and sometimes it feels like it might just swallow you whole. But at least it's alive. And that's something you can't fake—no matter how hard Ellicott City tries.

What do I carry from Ellicott City?

For me, Ellicott City is that place where I found some peace after moving from India in 2018. The streets here were slower, the pace of life gentler, and it offered a different rhythm than what I was used to in places like Gurgaon and Delhi. Here I could pause and reflect on the part of myself I was leaving behind and who I was becoming.

Living here, I've come to realize that it's not just about the quiet or the chaos of a place. Ellicott City holds a quiet authenticity that I didn't know I needed. After years of navigating the constant noise of cities like Delhi and Gurgaon, where everything seemed to be in perpetual motion, Ellicott City gave me the space to breathe. It taught me to slow down, to embrace the moments of stillness, and to appreciate the subtleties of life that are easy to overlook in a fast-paced environment.

But, like anywhere, it has its own challenges, its own undercurrents of expectation. It's easy to feel like everything needs to fit perfectly into place. But in Ellicott City, I've learned that it's okay for things to be silent. The peaceful streets and my restless mind—remind me that contradictions can exist side by side. I've realized that life is rarely as simple as it seems on the surface, and Ellicott City has taught me to accept that complexity. The town's calm, quaint charm contrasts sharply with the inner turbulence I sometimes feel, and that tension has shaped me in profound ways. I've learned that sometimes, the quiet, forces us to confront what we've been running from, and that it's only in those quiet moments that we truly find inner clarity.

Ellicott City has also helped me see that every place has its own story, even if it doesn't always show on the surface. The history embedded in its streets, the layers of experiences that have shaped it, have reflected back on me. I've learned that we're always navigating between what we want the world to be and what it really is. Sometimes, the mess and chaos are what help you find your truest self. And in that way, Ellicott City has become a reminder that the journey is rarely clean or easy, but that's where the real story is—inside the quiet, where we find who we really are.

Living here has shifted how I approach life. I came from a world that was fast and constantly changing, and moving here gave me the space to reflect on who I am beyond the hustle. I learned that it's not the world around you that defines you, but your ability to find peace with yourself in the midst of it all. Ellicott City has shaped me by showing me that balance is key— by teaching me to embrace both the quiet moments and the messy, chaotic ones. In doing so, I've learned to be more accepting of myself and the journey I'm on.

Washington D.C: Federal Façades

Washington, D.C. is the capital city of the United States, located on the East Coast, bordered by the states of Maryland and Virginia. It is just an hour away from Ellicott City where we live. For me and my family, it holds great historical and cultural significance, serving as a hub of politics, history, and culture. The city's blend of historic monuments, modern architecture, and the vibrancy of national decision-making, make it a place of inspiration and connection to the nation's past and future.

Monumental Detours

Driving from Ellicott City to Washington, D.C., feels like being drawn into the heart of something much bigger than yourself—and also like being pulled into a never-ending argument about the GPS. My dad's steady hands on the wheel don't waver, but his patience does every time the GPS chirps out instructions like, "Turn left in 500 feet," only to immediately shout, "Recalculating!" Mom, in the passenger seat, performs her routine of checking on my baby brother and sighing at the traffic like she's starring in a drama titled 'Why Did I Marry a Man Who Won't Ask for Directions'?

Ellicott City's serene, tree-lined streets quickly give way to the increasing chaos of D.C., but not before my elder sister, deep in her scrolling, looks up just long enough to declare, "This traffic is giving me anxiety," as if her earbuds weren't already blocking out 90% of the world's problems. My baby brother adds to the ambiance by throwing his stuffed elephant onto the floor for the seventh time, then protesting loudly when no one immediately retrieves it.

By the time the Washington Monument comes into view, I've counted at least three near-misses with merging cars and heard my dad mutter something suspiciously close to a swear word under his breath. And yet, despite the chaos, there's something electrifying about that first glimpse of D.C. It's like the city itself is daring you to keep up—though I swear even the monuments seem to judge us for the number of wrong turns we've taken.

D.C. isn't just a city; it's a well-dressed enigma that makes you question your footwear choices and why you thought bringing a stroller here was a good idea. As we drive by the Capitol Building, I wonder aloud if anyone inside is debating anything as important as whether or not we'll find parking before sundown. My dad's face is a mask of focus, my mom's already plotting the fastest route to coffee, and my elder sister is furiously texting about how her life is so much harder than everyone else's because her phone's battery is at 18%.

And yet, even amid the chaos, the city pulls you in. The buildings loom like they've seen it all, and the monuments stand tall like they know they're the real celebrities here. My baby brother stares wide-eyed at everything, possibly wondering if the Lincoln Memorial doubles as a playground. Meanwhile, I'm wondering if my dad will ever admit he's kind of impressed by the city, even if he'd rather be home, tinkering with the lawnmower in our suburban haven.

D.C. demands your attention—and your patience. As we inch closer to the National Mall, I can't help but marvel at the absurd beauty of it all: the history, the hope, the guy in the suit screaming into his Bluetooth earphones about quarterly projections, and the tourist group trying to take a selfie with a hot dog stand. It's a lot to take in, but somehow, it works. When we finally spot parking space, it feels like we've won some kind of urban survival game.

Stepping out of the car, we're greeted by the city's energy—a blend of ambition, history, and car horns. My mom immediately begins walking with purpose, dragging us along like she's on a mission to decode the Da Vinci Code. My dad stays behind, muttering about parking meters and the absurdity of $20 fees. The National Mall stretches before us, grand and iconic, as my sister snaps a picture while muttering, "Ugh, it's not even golden hour." My baby brother giggles at a pigeon, already more impressed by the wildlife than the Washington Monument. And me? I can't help but laugh at the sheer ridiculousness of it all. This isn't just a trip to D.C.; it's a full-on sitcom, starring my family and co-starring every wrong turn we took to get here.

Feeding the Capital

As we make our way deeper into Washington, D.C., food becomes more than just a necessity—it's an experience, a journey through the city's rich chapter of flavors, cultures, and stories. This is Washington, D.C., not just as a political capital but as a culinary one, where the food scene doesn't simply cater to tourists but speaks to the locals, the immigrants, the communities that have made this city their home. And we, the curious and the hungry, are here to listen. It's almost as if the food in D.C. has a secret life of its own, like the city's monuments but with a lot more spice and way less marble.

The adventure begins as we dive into the vibrancy of the National Mall, not for its monuments, but for the food trucks that line its paths, turning the city's heart into an international marketplace. It's as if the Mall got tired of being all dignified and decided to host a global food festival.

First up: Indian street food, and of course, Mom is the first to spot it. She orders *chole bhature* (spicy chickpeas gravy and crispy, soft deep-fried bread). Its aroma pulls us in. It's comforting, a taste of India in a new place. Mom smiles, tasting home again. I think she might start crying, but it's probably just the spices. My sister, though, heads straight for fusion food—Korean BBQ tacos; sweet, spicy, tangy, all wrapped in a tortilla. She offers me a bite, and I'm hooked. I know, I know, I came here for the monuments, but I've been sidetracked by the world of tacos. Sorry, Washington, D.C.—I have priorities. Dad sticks to a gourmet hot dog, topped with caramelized onions and artisanal mustard. He's unsure at first, but it surprises him. You can tell by the look on his face that he's questioning his entire life. And I can't blame him—who knew a hot dog could be so… introspective?

After the food trucks, we head to a bistro in Georgetown. Simple, fresh arugula salad, followed by roasted chicken— crispy, juicy, and satisfying. It's comfort food elevated. You can almost hear the chicken singing "I will survive" after being roasted to perfection. But D.C. is more than that. We try Ethiopian food in Adams Morgan: injera with spicy Doro Wat and lentil stew. The flavors are new but comforting, just like the city itself. It's the kind of meal that makes you think, "I have no idea what's going on here, but I'm in for the ride."

Later, we explore Chinatown. Dim sum with steamed dumplings, crispy spring rolls, and soft buns. Even Dad is content. Yes, you read that right—Dad is at peace, which is a rare and beautiful sight. The world is finally in harmony. D.C.'s food isn't just about filling up; it's about connection—to culture, history, and the diversity that defines the city. Every bite surprises, challenges, and invites you to discover something new, whether you're into history, politics, or just finding a new favorite taco. Who knew D.C. was so profound?

Shopping Marvels: D.C. Edition

Shopping in Washington, D.C. is like a game of hide-and-seek, except the hiding part is done by the fashion, and the seeking is a bit of a chaotic disaster. For a family like mine, it's the one time we all temporarily agree that spending money on stuff we don't need is actually a bonding activity. The five of us—my parents, my elder sister, my baby brother, and me—rarely find common ground on anything, but somehow, we all stumble into this mess of consumerism together, like a misplaced family photo in a department store catalog.

The drive from Ellicott City to D.C. starts off peacefully, like a normal suburban trip. But the closer we get, the more it feels like we're entering a pressure cooker where everyone's fashion insecurities bubble to the surface. As we inch closer to Georgetown, the suburban calm gets replaced with the sharp buzz of the city. You can literally feel the air change as if the city itself is saying, "Welcome to the place where your credit card balance will never be the same."

As we park and step onto the cobblestones of Georgetown, the whole place reeks of history, or maybe it's just the vintage coffee shops, but either way, it smells like money. My sister bolts ahead, clearly on a mission to find something that'll make her look like a chic version of an influencer who can still say "I'm just like you, but I shop at places you've never heard of." She steps into this boutique with a minimalistic facade, and I swear, the air inside actually gets thinner. There's a subtle warning on the door: "Enter with taste, leave with your self-esteem intact." She picks up a blouse made of silk and embroidery so fancy it probably requires a personal invitation to wear. As she holds it up, you'd think she was evaluating whether this blouse could pass a test for international diplomacy.

Then, there's Mom. She's the opposite of my sister—she's looking for the kind of things that make you think, "Do I need this? Do I need to know where this came from?" Mom slides into an artisan shop with shelves stacked high with pottery, woven textiles, and necklaces made out of rocks that probably have backstories more interesting than my entire life. She's all about things that speak to her, and when she picks up a wooden box, you can practically hear her thinking, "This is going to fit perfectly in the living room, next to that vase no one ever notices." That's how she shops: not for the glory, but for the subtle home decor flex that makes her feel like the world is a little more beautiful.

Dad, on the other hand, is still stuck in the "I just want to sit down" phase of the shopping experience. He's pacing near the door, looking like he's contemplating the meaning of life while checking his watch. Then, a miracle happens. He spots a small, dusty vintage electronics shop wedged between a wine bar and a paper boutique. It's like the Universe opened a door just for him. I follow him inside, and instantly, it smells like a mixture of old vinyl records and regret. Dad stands in front of a turntable like it's the Holy Grail. He picks up a vinyl record, squints at it, and I'm half convinced he's going to buy it and start his own collection of music that only plays on equipment you have to carefully dust every week. But no, after a quick moment of contemplation (read: pretending to be a hipster), he puts it down, muttering something about how the record's "too new" for his taste, and exits.

Next up is CityCenterDC, the shopping district that feels like it was designed by the world's richest architect who couldn't care less if you were impressed. The stores here ooze wealth in a way that makes you feel like you're being judged for looking at the price tag. My sister sprints from one store to the next, and I'm honestly surprised no one's tried to hire her as a personal shopper. She walks past the fancy storefronts like she owns them, the glass doors parting for her as she's drawn to the high-end fashion brands. She tries on some oversized sunglasses that make her look like a celebrity on a mission, and then she pulls one of those moves where she turns in front of the mirror like she's auditioning for America's Next Top Model. It's not the sunglasses she wants; it's the aura of sheer, unearned confidence that comes with them.

Meanwhile, Dad is in "I'm just here for the snacks" mode, trailing behind, and my baby brother is having the time of his life—pointing at things he doesn't know the name of but assumes are important. He's basically living in his own world, where the concept of "luxury" is limited to a plush toy he can shove into his mouth.

Finally, we hit Pentagon City Mall, where the vibe shifts from "Look at me, I'm rich" to "Look at me, I'm a bargain hunter." Here, it's all about the deals and chaos. Mom's back on the hunt for things that "fill the spaces in our lives," but she's doing it in a store that's more crowded than a Black Friday Sale. My sister is still on the lookout for the next statement piece, flipping through clothes like she's solving a Rubik's Cube. Dad, predictably, finds a bench, sighs dramatically, and watches us like we're an elaborate circus performance. My baby brother, on the other hand, is just as entertained by a set of plastic blocks as he is by the entire Mall of America. If there's a toy section, he's going to investigate it like it's the most fascinating archaeological dig of all time. He has zero interest in what we're doing—he just wants to touch everything.

As the Sun sets and the city shifts from tourist central to "Let's go home and pretend we didn't spend too much," we leave the mall, heads spinning, wallets a little lighter, but with enough stories to last a lifetime. Shopping in D.C. isn't about the things we buy—it's about the ridiculous things that happen while we try to act like we know what we're doing. For us, it's just another chapter in the family comedy that never really ends.

Midnight Confessions

Washington, D.C. at night isn't just a city; it's like the city has had too many shots of espresso and is now trying to convince everyone it's totally fine, just living its best life. Gone is the pristine, politician-approved glamour of the daytime. Instead, the city feels a little less like the Capitol Hill stage and more like a secret club where nobody really wants to admit they're a member. The grand monuments become silhouettes in the background, and the people? Well, they're just stumbling through their own little dramas like they're auditioning for a reality TV show.

Our night kicks off in Dupont Circle, where the streetlights throw just enough light to make you feel like you're in a low- budget thriller, but it's also somehow charming. We duck into a café that looks like it's trying to survive the apocalypse—its neon sign flickers like it's had one too many bad nights. Inside though, it's warm. Warm enough like, 'I swear I had come here to get work done, but now I just want to fall asleep.' The lighting is the color of the Sun setting over a latte you didn't ask for but will drink anyway because you're too polite to ask for water. The conversations around us are whispers, almost like people are holding auditions for 'World's Most Subtle Confession.'

At our corner table, we take it all in with a cocktail of curiosity and mild judgment. There's a woman at the bar typing like the future of humanity depends on it. Her fingers fly across the keyboard with so much energy it could power the whole city for a week. She glances at the window every few seconds like she's waiting for someone, or a taxi, or a dramatic plot twist.

Then there's the guy in the leather jacket, nursing a cup of coffee like it's the last drop of warmth he'll ever experience. He's alone, but not in a romantic, 'I'm just here to vibe' kind of way. More like a 'I've seen some stuff, but not enough to make me interesting at parties' kind of way. He's basically marinating in his own past, which is fine—until his jacket starts looking like it might take over the entire café.

Then enters a young man, dressed in a suit that's sharp enough to give you a paper cut. He's moving like he's running out of time, which, you know, probably is true. He orders coffee with the urgency of someone who thinks caffeine might be the answer to everything and watches the barista like they're about to announce the winning lottery numbers. He takes a seat, scanning the room like he's lost his phone and is now hoping to find it under someone else's table. Spoiler: he won't. The café, with its hidden stories and half-spoken thoughts, feels like a brief moment in a much larger game of 'Who's trying to have a breakdown in public this time?'

As we step back into the night, the city does its best impersonation of a bad drama. People are rushing by with purpose, looking like they've got places to go—whether those places are good places or bad ones, who knows? There's a woman marching down the street, holding a stack of papers like she's just discovered her secret identity and needs to get away right now. A group of teenagers laughs loudly on a bench, their conversation a chaotic symphony of high school optimism. It's like the city forgot that some people still haven't been chewed up by the machine yet. They're just out there, throwing out jokes about school and how maybe they'll save the planet by next Friday. As they talk over one another, the city seems just a tiny bit lighter, like it's on the verge of a comedic breakthrough. At the waterfront, a violinist plays like he's one bad day away from releasing a grunge album. His music drifts through the air, so dramatic it almost feels like he's trying to make a point, but it's unclear exactly what that point is. People drop change into his case, but it feels less like generosity and more like people are passing the buck—like the music is somehow their problem now. He's there, playing for an audience that pretends they understand music, but somehow, everyone walks away.

In the end, as we drive back to Ellicott City, I can't help but think about D.C.'s after-dark personality. It's messy, chaotic, and just a little too alive for its own good. The people we saw at the café, on the streets, by the waterfront—all of them are part of some larger, absurd mosaic that probably makes way more sense if you squint. At night, Washington, D.C. is like a giant, slightly dysfunctional family dinner—full of ambition, confusion, and everyone trying to figure out if they should just get dessert and go home.

If Washington were a person...

If Washington, D.C. were a person, it would be a dignified statesman, the kind of figure who commands respect not through sheer force but through an effortless blend of authority and sophistication. Picture him in a sharp, tailored suit that fits as if it were made just for him—classic, understated, yet undeniably powerful. His every move exudes a kind of restrained confidence, a mastery of the art of presence. He walks with purpose, each step deliberate, as if he's always navigating through a sea of expectations and implications. There's a practiced elegance in his demeanor, the kind that suggests a life lived in the corridors of power, where every glance, every gesture, is laden with some intention. His speech is a symphony of measured tones and carefully chosen words, designed to both impress and persuade. He speaks with the gravitas of someone who's seen it all, who understands the weight of every decision and the ripple effects they create.

In public, this statesman is the epitome of poise and control. His speeches are delivered with a charisma that captures the attention of all who listen, his rhetoric both inspiring and reassuring. He is the embodiment of the city's grandeur, reflecting its role as the center of power and influence. His presence is a blend of classic authority and modern charm, a representation of the city's complex identity.

Yet, behind closed doors, the statesman's life is far more intricate. The pressure of his role is palpable, the weight of his decisions a constant companion. Here, he grapples with the more personal and less visible aspects of his influence—conversations that shape policy, decisions that impact lives, and moments of doubt that rarely see the light of day. He's a figure of contradictions, managing to maintain a façade of unflappable calm while navigating the tumultuous currents of political and social responsibility.

The statesman's interactions with those around him are a study in diplomacy and negotiation. With allies, he is a source of support and wisdom, his guidance both strategic and empathetic. With adversaries, he is the epitome of tact and firmness, his ability to balance respect with assertiveness a testament to his skill. His demeanor is a blend of patience and resolve, reflecting his deep understanding of the delicate balance required in his role.

In his private time, the statesman might be found in a quiet corner of a sophisticated lounge, his reflection a mix of contemplation and weariness. Here, away from the public eye, the weight of his responsibilities is more apparent. The decisions that keep him up at night, the delicate negotiations, and the countless interactions that shape his day all come to the forefront. It's a space where the public façade of calm gives way to the more complex, and often more vulnerable, realities of his role.

The city's landmarks—its grand buildings, historic monuments, and bustling avenues—serve as a backdrop to the statesman's life. They are symbols of his influence, standing as testament to the legacy he represents. But it's in the quieter moments, in the unspoken interactions and the personal reflections, where the true depth of his character is revealed.

Washington, D.C., as embodied by this dignified statesman, is a place of power and prestige, of history and ambition. As he moves through the city, his presence is both a guiding force and a reflection of its essence. It is a city that thrives on both the visible and the hidden, where every action and decision carries weight, and where the past and present intersect in a complex dance of influence and legacy.

From City Lights to Suburban Nights

As we leave Washington, D.C., heading back toward Ellicott City, the drive feels like we're taking a cosmic detour from one universe to another—one moment we're amidst the relentless energy of the city, and the next, we're pulling into a time warp to a quieter, more peaceful place where even the trees seem to breathe slower. The city's vibrant hum becomes a distant memory as the headlights slice through the night, like we're erasing the chaos behind us, mile by mile.

The streets of D.C. blur out of existence as we drive; its once vivid lights melting into a soft blur, like a city that's blinking out after a long night of being awake. Each mile further feels like we're peeling away a layer of some grand city cake, only to find ourselves staring at the simplicity of suburban frosting. We're leaving behind the weight of Washington's towering ambition and entering the realm of suburban calm, where the pace of life doesn't feel like it's in a rush to finish its 1,000 things at once.

Dad is driving with the focus of a man who sees every red light as a personal challenge, Mom with her eyes seeing through the window, holding on to the last breath of city lights, as if she's trying to store them up in some secret corner of her memory for later. Meanwhile, my sister and I are squished in the back, sharing that exact kind of silence where you both feel like you're on the same page but no one's talking. It's the kind of silence that, in retrospect, probably has some deep metaphor about the city we've just left, but we're too tired to unpack it right now.

The further we leave behind Washington, the more the world outside transforms. The buildings get shorter, the roads get more widened, and you start thinking that maybe we just left the world's biggest game of Tetris behind and now we're in the "scenic route" of life. There's a slow sort of calm that replaces the jittery intensity of D.C., a place where every corner had a hustle, a deal, a person talking too loud on their phone. But now? The sounds outside the car are softer, like the world's trying to hush itself for the night. There's an occasional house light that flickers in the distance, like it's sending us a note that says, "Hey, welcome back to normal."

The city's shrill, constant hum? Gone. Replaced by the gentle murmur of suburban life, where things happen at a pace so slow it could be mistaken for an art form. We're on the final stretch now—Ellicott City looms ahead like a welcome mat to a world of lawns and neighbors who don't all seem to be in a rush to do anything. It's like the city was the high-speed roller coaster, and now we're settling into a comfy, if not slightly slower, Ferris Wheel ride. The towering buildings of D.C. are replaced by cute little houses with their own quirks, set far enough apart to suggest that no one's going to knock on your door at 2 a.m. with an urgent "I need you to sign something."

Finally, as we pull into our driveway, there's this satisfying sense of return. Washington's chaotic, layered personality lingers in my mind—like a sticky memory—but here, in the calm of Ellicott City, things feel... still. The stories of Washington only exist as distant echoes now. There's no more buzzing energy, no faces trying to hide their stories behind subway tiles. Here, the stories are quieter, more introspective, and, dare I say, more peaceful. It's like we're living in the background of a bigger, louder world, and we just got home to the quiet part.

What do I carry from Washington D.C.?

The drive from Ellicott City to Washington, D.C. isn't just a change of scenery—it's a reminder of how we navigate the spaces between calm and chaos. Ellicott City represents the quiet, predictable moments of life, where the rhythm is slower, and the pace is gentler. In contrast,

D.C. pulses with energy and constant movement, a place where the streets seem to buzz with purpose, and the skyline reflects ambition and progress.

Moving between these two worlds mirrors the challenge we all face: balancing the peaceful and the chaotic, the quiet and the loud. It's a push and pull between two very different energies, each one valuable in its own way. It's easy to feel torn, pulled in different directions—yearning for the stillness of Ellicott City, only to be swept up by the frenetic pace of D.C.

The message here is simple: life isn't always about choosing between two extremes, but about how we handle the tension between them. The calm moments, like those I find in Ellicott City, teach us about reflection and self-awareness. They give us space to breathe, think, and reconnect with ourselves. These moments of stillness ground me, reminding me to pause, even when the world outside is rushing ahead. But then, there's D.C.—a place where the chaos forces us to adapt, grow, and find our place in the world. The city's pace, its constant movement, challenges me to be resilient, to embrace change, and to stay grounded despite the whirlwind around me. What matters is how we embrace both sides of life. It's about how we use both the calm and the chaos to shape who we are. The real lesson is that life isn't about seeking perfection or avoiding struggle—it's about finding a balance between the stillness and the movement.

The journey from Ellicott City to D.C. is a metaphor for the constant flow between these two forces. Embrace the calm when you can, but don't shy away from the chaos—it's where you'll find your true path. Both have something to offer; both are necessary. It's in that balance that we grow stronger, clearer, and more authentic.

Baltimore: Where Grit meets Grace

Baltimore is located in the state of Maryland, right along the Chesapeake Bay on the East Coast of the United States. Just about 40 miles northeast of Washington, D.C., it sits in the heart of the Mid- Atlantic region, offering a perfect mix of maritime history and urban vibrance. The city's proximity to Washington D.C. gives it a unique blend of cultural diversity, historical significance, and modern energy.

For me, Baltimore was always just a short 20-minute drive away from Ellicott City, but it felt like a world apart. Ellicott City, with its peaceful suburban streets, offered quiet comfort—wide roads, manicured lawns, and a calm that sometimes felt almost too still. But when we needed a change of pace, a little action, or simply a reminder that the world was buzzing out there, we'd head to Baltimore. The city was alive, constantly moving, with vibrant streets, bustling markets, and endless possibilities for adventure. Whether it was walking around the Inner Harbor, grabbing a bite of fresh seafood, or getting lost in the city's energy, Baltimore was the place that always had something new to offer.

Arriving: Baltimore's Bold Hug of Chaos

Baltimore doesn't introduce itself politely. It doesn't wave across the room, offer a handshake, or even ask if you have dietary restrictions. Instead, it throws the door open, tosses you a steaming plate of crabs, and says, "Here, figure it out!" It's not a city you visit—it's a city that demands you hold on tight, while it takes you for a ride.

Our first encounter with Baltimore in 2018 was nothing short of legendary. Our navy-blue Toyota Camry—a vehicle Dad worshipped with such fervor, it might as well be parked in a temple—glided hesitantly down unfamiliar streets. It was our voyage away from the suburban calm of Ellicott City, where the biggest commotion was the occasional jogger forgetting to pick up after their dog.

I was eleven, perched in the backseat with the wide-eyed wonder of someone who hadn't yet seen a city that looked alive in the way Baltimore did—messy, sprawling, chaotic, and undeniably proud of itself. Beside me, my elder sister sat scrolling on her phone, the light glowing from the screen making her look like a very bored oracle. "Are we there yet?" She mumbled nonchalantly, never once lifting her eyes. Up front, Mom was the picture of composed determination, gripping her phone's GPS like she'd just been handed state secrets. Dad, however, was gripping the steering wheel like it owed him money, muttering about "left exits" and "unnecessary roundabouts" in a tone that suggested he might write a strongly worded letter to the Department of Transportation.

As we neared the city, the scenery morphed. The gentle lawns and cookie-cutter houses of Ellicott City gave way to tightly packed rowhouses painted in every color imaginable—brick reds, baby blues, bright yellows. Some had fresh coats of paint, standing tall like soldiers in formation. Others were weathered, their shutters hanging askew like they'd partied too hard the night before. And then, the skyline. It wasn't just a cluster of buildings; it was a declaration - "We're here! And we dare you to look away!" It wasn't the polished, glittering skyline of a corporate city. No, this one wore its rough edges like a badge of honor, like it was saying, "Yeah, we've been through some stuff. You got a problem with that?"

When we reached the heart of Baltimore, it felt like we'd entered a different universe. The streets bustled with energy, people jaywalked with confidence bordering on defiance, and the air seemed to hum with possibility—or maybe just the fumes from the food trucks on every corner.

I felt as if the spirit of Baltimore saying to me: "Take me as I am, kiddo. And wipe that look off your face; you're in my house now!"

Food: Baltimore's Edible Love Letter

If Baltimore were a dish, it wouldn't be fancy or delicate. It would be messy, bold, and utterly unforgettable. Dad had made it his life's mission to find the city's best crab cakes. He would treat every restaurant like it's a contestant in a high-stakes cooking competition, dissecting each bite with the precision of a food critic and the enthusiasm of a man who treats good seafood as a sacred spiritual experience. Lexington Market would be his holy ground. He would order crab cakes with the kind of reverence usually reserved for national monuments. "This…" he would announce with his food still stuffed in his mouth, "is how crab cakes are supposed to taste!"

But Baltimore's culinary delights didn't stop at crab cakes. There was fried fish so crispy it crunched loud enough to turn heads, and spicy crab soup that felt like a warm hug from the inside.

And then there were snowballs—an unapologetically sugary treat that was less "dessert" and more "pure joy in a cup!" We'd sit on the curb with our brightly colored cups, syrup staining our tongues and napkins flapping in the breeze. There was nothing elegant about it, and that was the point. Eating a snowball was a declaration that sometimes, life's sweetest moments come with sticky fingers and stained shirts.

Shopping: The Family Olympics

Shopping in Baltimore is not for the faint-hearted; it's a sport, an art form, and occasionally, a battle of wills.

Dad approaches every purchase like he's negotiating a business deal. Shoes, for example, are thoroughly inspected for sole quality, arch support, and bounce. "A bad shoe can ruin your life," he says with the gravity of someone delivering a TED Talk. Mom, on the other hand, is a master haggler. Watching her bargain with street vendors is like watching a live performance of Gladiator. She'll start with a smile, throw in a compliment, and end with a price so low you'd think she just invented reverse inflation. My sister treats shopping like a strategic campaign, each purchase a carefully chosen weapon in her ongoing quest for world domination—or at least Instagram domination.

By the end of the day, we're all loaded down with bags, exhausted but victorious. Dad beams over his "best purchase ever," Mom recounts her bargaining triumphs, and my sister admires her new accessories like they're pieces in an art gallery. Me? I just enjoy the snacks. Because if there's one thing Baltimore knows how to do, it's make you feel full—in every sense of the word.

People: Charm City's Cast of Characters

If Baltimore were a stage, its people would be the stars, the understudies, and the stagehands—all at once. They're not just part of the city's story; they are the story.

Take the aged man who's always perched on his stoop, sipping coffee out of a mug that might be older than he is. His nod isn't just a greeting—it's a rite of passage. It says, "You're here now. Don't mess it up." His coffee, I suspect, is less caffeine and more liquid wisdom, brewed strong enough to wake the ancestors.

Then there are the kids playing basketball in the alley. Their game isn't just about points—it's about pride, about saying, "Yeah, this is our court, cracks and all. You got a problem with that?" The ball bounces off the walls with a rhythm that feels like it's part of the city's heartbeat.

And the artists? Oh, they're everywhere. Painting murals on crumbling buildings, turning forgotten corners into explosions of color and meaning. One mural we pass regularly features a woman's face, her eyes fierce and knowing. It's like she's looking directly at you and saying, "What's your excuse?"

And of course, the city wouldn't be complete without its moms. These women are forces of nature, juggling grocery bags, toddlers, and existential dread like they're auditioning for a reality show called "Survivor: Baltimore Edition." Watching my own mom navigate this city feels like watching a superhero origin story. "You can't let the world see you sweat," she says, balancing five bags of vegetables in one hand and my brother in the other.

If Baltimore were a person...

If Baltimore were a person, it would be a scrappy, street-smart entrepreneur—someone who's seen it all and refuses to back down. It's a city that doesn't smooth its edges or polish its surface. Instead, it wears its scars with pride, a testament to everything it has endured and everything it continues to fight for.

The Inner Harbor, with its shimmering waters and historic ships, feels like Baltimore at its most polished. It's where tourists flock, cameras in hand, eager to capture the city's best angles. But venture a few blocks away, and the story shifts. The cobblestone streets of Fells Point, the vibrant murals of Station North, the worn facades of West Baltimore—these are the places where the city's true character reveals itself.

Baltimore is a city of contrasts – where grit meets grace, and resilience dances with restlessness. It's a place where beauty exists in the cracks and corners, in the faded murals and the graffiti that doubles as art.

Baltimore doesn't ask for your approval. It doesn't try to win you over. But if you take the time to see it, to really see it, you'll find a city that's as complex and compelling as any story ever told.

Leaving

Leaving Baltimore never really felt like leaving. It was more like pressing pause on something unfinished. Every time we drove out of the city—past the packed rowhouses and the fading murals—it felt like we were stepping away from a place that still had more to show us.

The ride back to Ellicott City was always quieter. Not because the roads were calm, but because we were. Tired from the day, maybe a little sun-drenched, maybe still thinking about something we'd seen or heard—Baltimore had a way of leaving you deep in thought. No one talked much. We didn't have to. The city had already said enough.

What do I carry from Baltimore?

Baltimore wasn't just a city we visited—it was a place that shaped how we saw the world and, in many ways, how we saw each other. In Baltimore's energy, I found something that I hadn't expected to feel—a sense of belonging not in spite of its chaos, but because of it. The city was a reflection of how life doesn't always follow a straight line. Its unpredictability, its mix of cultures, and its ability to surprise at every corner taught me to embrace the unpredictability of life itself. The chaos wasn't something to be controlled; it was something to be lived, felt, and appreciated for all its messy beauty.

Baltimore shaped me by showing me that there's value in stepping outside of the quiet comfort of Ellicott City. While Ellicott City gave me peace and space to reflect, Baltimore taught me that home needn't always be quiet; it could be loud, messy, and full of energy, and yet, it could support your growth.

For my family, Baltimore has always been a place where we would come to connect—with the city, with each other and with ourselves. It's a place that forces us to confront our own contradictions, to see the ways we are both shaped by our past and defined by our future.

Epilogue

The places we live are more than just settings; they shape us in ways we often don't realize until we look back. This book was an attempt to do just that: to reflect on how these places have defined who I am. Every city, town, and in-between places have left its mark on me—lessons, emotions, and memories scattered like breadcrumbs across the map of my life.

Delhi was a city of chaos and contradictions. The city's constant motion demanded adaptability and resilience. Its contrasts—ancient monuments beside glass skyscrapers, street vendors alongside luxury cars—reflected the contradictions within myself. Living in Delhi taught me to navigate these dualities and find moments of beauty amid chaos. It showed me how to appreciate fleeting kindness and adapt to relentless change. The city's energy pushed me to grow, while its fleeting pauses reminded me of the value of empathy.

Gurgaon's outwardly perfect image made me understand how easy it was to get lost in the pursuit of admiration and status, only to realize that the emptiness of that chase is far more profound than the fleeting satisfaction of success. It taught me to question the idea of success and wealth as ultimate goals. It taught me that there's more to life than the glittering façade and that real satisfaction comes not from impressing others, but from being true to myself and cultivating meaningful relationships.

Darbhanga felt like stepping into another world—one rooted in nature and tradition. My *Nani's* house, with its veranda overlooking the pond, was alive with family and history. Every meal, festival, and prayer carried the weight of generations. Here, I learned about continuity and the strength of roots. But Darbhanga also posed a challenge: reconciling the simplicity of life there with my growing aspirations. It taught me to honor where I came from, even as I dreamed of a future that looked entirely different. The rhythms of Darbhanga remind me that holding onto my roots doesn't tether me—it grounds me.

Bokaro was a world of purpose and rhythm, where life revolved around the steel factories that fueled the city. Dad's work embodied the values of hard work and pride, even though I was too young to fully grasp the depth of his sacrifices. Visiting Bokaro, I learned the value of routine. The hum of industry set the pace of life, instilling in me a sense of discipline and drive. But it also revealed its softer side in the evenings, when jasmine-filled air and open spaces provided moments of peace. It taught me balance—the coexistence of hard work and quiet reflection. The lessons of Bokaro remained with me: respect for effort, an appreciation for beauty even in gritty experiences, and the drive to move forward with purpose.

Padri was our family's roots—a village where time seemed to stretch endlessly, and where extended family ties bound the community together. Here, people shared their histories, joys, and sorrows with patience and care. Yet, beneath the warmth lay a quiet hesitation, a reluctance to fully trust. Past betrayals and lingering wounds had taught the people of Padri that trust must be earned through time, and small consistent acts. This duality shaped my understanding of relationships. Community wasn't just about proximity— it was about investing the time to truly see and understand each other. Despite the unspoken distance that lingered between people, their willingness to give time and care, created bonds that were slow to build but deeply lasting. Padri taught me that trust was fragile, but its strength lay in the patience to nurture it.

Ellicott City offered something I hadn't realized I craved: stillness. Its quiet streets and rolling hills allowed me to breathe, to reflect, to simply be. Here, life felt less like a race and more like a journey. Here, I learned to value the small rituals of everyday life—walking along trails, visiting farmers' markets, and finding joy in quiet moments. Growth doesn't have to be loud or dramatic, and sometimes the quietest places leave the deepest impact.

Washington, D.C., with its stately monuments and grand avenues, was a city that inspired ambition. Walking through the National Mall or standing before the Lincoln Memorial, I felt a deep connection to ideals larger than myself. D.C. taught me to dream big and to see ambition as not just personal but a way to contribute to something greater. It reminded me that the power of possibility lay in daring to believe in it.

Baltimore was a city of resilience, where every street told a story of struggle and triumph. Its gritty docks and vibrant neighborhoods embodied a beauty born of imperfection. Baltimore taught me that strength wasn't just about enduring challenges but thriving because of them. It reminded me that true grit comes from facing hardship head-on, with grace and determination.

Each place in my story has shaped me in its own way. They are all strokes in a painting of who I am. Together, they've taught me to navigate life with resilience, empathy, and a sense of purpose.

Acknowledgment

This book has been a journey one filled with learning, rewriting, reflecting, and growing. The process was not just about putting words on a page, but about shaping thoughts, discovering clarity, and honoring truth.

I am deeply grateful to Milind Jakati, my editor, for his thoughtful guidance and unwavering commitment to refining this work. A heartfelt thank you to Jonely Godhino for beautifully formatting the manuscript with care and precision, and to Pramod Khera for believing in my voice and giving this book a platform to reach the world. I sincerely appreciate Pankhuri Shukla for her constant encouragement and. guidance throughout this journey.

To my parents and family, your love has been my foundation. Every word here carries your support between the lines.

To my readers—thank you for joining me on this path. It's your curiosity, your willingness to think deeply, and your belief in ideas that give this work life beyond the page.

And to everyone who touched this process in ways seen or unseen—thank you.